Sitting in Isaiah

The Spiritual Spa

A Bible Study Devotional

By Yvonne Wolf

Sitting in Isaiah

ISBN: 978-1-935252-51-1
© 2009 Yvonne Wolf

All rights reserved. No part of this book may be reproduced in any form without the express written consent of the author and the publisher, except for the inclusion of brief quotations in review.

All scripture quotations, unless otherwise indicated, are taken from the Holy Bible, New International Version®, NIV®. Copyright ©1973, 1978, 1984 by Biblica, Inc.™ Used by permission of Zondervan. All rights reserved worldwide.

Scripture quotations marked :NKJV™" are taken from the New King James Version®. Copyright © 1982 by Thomas Nelson, Inc. Used by permission. All rights reserved.

Scripture quotations marked "THE MESSAGE" are taken from The Message, The Bible in Contemporary Language (THE MESSAGE) published by NavPress, © 1993, 1994, 1995, 1996, 2000, 2001, 2002. Used by Permission of NavPress, All Rights Reserved. www.navpress.com (1-800-366-7788).

Published By One More Chapter Publishing

© Belonging to Him Ministries 2009. All rights reserved.

Sitting in Isaiah

For my husband Jeff,
For encouraging me to answer God's call,
for helping to bring this book to life and
for loving me as we journey together.

© Belonging to Him Ministries 2009. All rights reserved.

Sitting in Isaiah

Table of Contents

Introduction 6

Chapter One 13

Chapter Two 27

Chapter Three 43

Chapter Four 61

Chapter Five 79

Chapter Six 93

Chapter Seven 109

Chapter Eight 127

Chapter Nine 139

Chapter Ten 153

Bibliography 167

© Belonging to Him Ministries 2009. All rights reserved.

Introduction

Sitting in Isaiah

Looking back, I can't quite remember the specific incident that led me to the conclusion that I was in desperate need of a spa get-away! The revelation came at a particularly stressful time in my life. Life's disappointments, financial difficulties, losses, health issues, busyness and depression had ravaged my soul to an all time low. My soul had been scorched many times in the past and I had always been able to rebuild and rebound. But this time it was more devastating and I just couldn't get myself together. I desperately wanted to run away to a spa for a few weeks even though I knew I had neither the time nor the money. As I sought the Lord for a rest from my life and some time to be rejuvenated, He answered in His usual unexpected way by taking me to a spa all right! He led me to experience a spiritual spa in the book of Isaiah!

Sitting in Isaiah: The Spiritual Spa developed out of my own need for and experience of spiritual rejuvenation and restoration. Written as a daily Bible study and devotional, it focuses on the ten selected chapters from the book of Isaiah that spoke most to me, with five lessons from each passage. Each lesson is intended to be completed in one "sitting" or *daily quiet time*, and readers will find the greatest benefit from completing the lessons in five consecutive days. I have found that by sitting and abiding in the same passage for five days in a row, wonderful things begin to happen in our spiritual development:
- we become more familiar with God through His Word and better able to "hear" Him speaking to us and our life situation
- we get the opportunity to soak in and actually learn God's truth and make it a part of us, and His Word changes our lives as it moves from our heads to our hearts
- we fortify and strengthen the life change God brings by memorizing key verses that clearly express His truth to us, storing them up for future reminders and use by the Holy Spirit

The unselected chapters of Isaiah are also included in this study as an optional one-chapter-per-day reading plan. Those who can include a full reading of Isaiah while completing the Spiritual Spa lessons will be blessed by gaining a fuller context of the life and times of this amazing major prophet and man of God. Many additional rich treasures of truth are waiting to be found there by those who seek them. My hope and prayer is that this record of my own experience and lessons learned will benefit and encourage any who are weary to recover their lives.

It is challenging to find quality time to meet with God. Life is busy, with the added stress of illness, loss, fatigue, anxiety, children, spouses, friends and family, along with work, deadlines and depression. God wants our time with Him to be a respite from the burdens of life, and not an added burden. He doesn't put anything on us that won't fit - I love that! We all want clothing that fits us properly. Just think how well God wants our time with Him to fit us!

Matthew 11:28-30 from THE MESSAGE says it best. *"Are you tired? Worn out? Burned out on religion? Come to me. Get away with me and you'll recover your life. I'll show you how to take a real rest. Walk with me and work with me—watch how I do it. Learn the unforced rhythms of grace. I won't lay anything heavy or ill-fitting on you. Keep company with me and you'll learn to live freely and lightly"*.

Since everything and everyone in our lives are affected by our relationship with God, we

Sitting in Isaiah

should put the highest priority on meeting with Him. We cannot be a healthy person having healthy relationships without being filled up with the Spirit of God. Being filled with the Spirit is the goal of our time with God. We receive the Holy Spirit when we accept Jesus Christ as our Savior. The Spirit is everpresent thereafter as God's seal upon us, but how much the Spirit fills us depends upon our willingness to be filled.

Study Guide for *Sitting in Isaiah, Bible Study Devotional*

Set a time for your quiet time when you are at your best. Even though you might not consider yourself to be a "morning person", consider trying to meet Him in the morning when you first wake. Over the years my "non-morning students" have confessed to me that the best time to meet with God *is* first thing in the morning. Once we get into our day it is very hard to put the brakes on, stop and have a quiet time. Beginning our day with God is the greatest demonstration that He is our first priority. If you aren't a morning person, ask God to help you to meet with Him then anyway. When you get up, stay up and fight the temptation to crawl back into bed! Keep the **same time** every day as frequently as possible. This helps you to establish a comfortable routine. Please don't feel any guilt if you have chosen to have your quiet time later in the day. What matters to Him is that you are making time for Him, period.

When Jeff and I first married, he regularly sought to have his quiet times in the evenings, since he wasn't really a morning person. But as his career and our family grew it became increasingly more difficult to have evening quiet times. I watched God teach Jeff to carve out morning time for a quiet time. Now my husband begins each day in a business meeting with God. He believes that everything in his business and his life is directly impacted by his time with his heavenly Father.

When our children were young I found my best time with God to be in the mornings after breakfast. I would sit in our children's play room, open the Word and spend time journaling my prayers to Him as my children played. As our children grew so did my taxi driving responsibilities. Mornings grew to be very hectic getting three children off to school so I found my best time for a quiet time to be in my car, while waiting to pick up our kids. I learned a powerful lesson during those demanding days as a mother of young children: God is able to speak to my heart in the midst of what seems like chaos around me. Though it works best to find a quiet place, God is realistic and understands our responsibilities. He honored my heart's desire to be with Him in spite of my noisy busy life.

Pick a place that is comfortable and free from distractions, and return to the **same place** for your quiet time everyday whenever possible.

After you decide on the best place and time for sitting with the Lord, you are ready to gather your quiet time supplies. It might be a good idea to use a book bag, satchel or perhaps like me you would enjoy a nicely decorated basket to keep them handy. Here is a list of suggested quiet time supplies:
- Bibles, both a study Bible (with a concordance and study helps), and a modern day

© Belonging to Him Ministries 2009. All rights reserved.

Sitting in Isaiah

language version such as *The Message* or *The Living Bible*.
- a journal for recording prayers and conversations with God
- devotionals to provide structure, encourage and give direction - must be Bible based, and encourage you to dig deeper into the Bible
- index cards for recording key verses on for meditation and memorization
- sticky notes to write yourself reminders that you think of during this time, so that you can put them aside for later and avoid interrupting your devotions
- tissues, pens and highlighters

Keep a spiritual journal during your quiet times. Spiritual journaling is recording your spiritual journey; it is not a diary. You might enjoy keeping a diary, but journaling has a different purpose. Each day's lesson in *Sitting in Isaiah* gives space for journaling your thoughts and prayers to God.

The focus of a spiritual journal is truth about God and your relationship to Him. Journaling during your quiet times will help you recall the truth you are learning and creates a record to look back upon, as well as helping to focus your thoughts during your quiet time. Recording truth focuses us on Jesus and His solutions for us rather than our problems and the magnitude of them. Recording our reflections about that truth also helps us meditate upon it and decipher how to apply that truth to our life. Emotions are important, but we must guard against over-focusing on our emotions when keeping our spiritual journal.

Emotions are not truth that we should live by. In her book *A Different Kind of Wild,* Debbie Alsdorf says, "There is a different way to live, and the Bible calls this different life *living up*. Living up means a change in focus and direction. Living up moves us from a focus on what we are feeling or what is immediately in front of us to an upward focus on committing our stray thoughts and emotions to God." She adds, "we were born to live up instead of settling for being dragged down by our emotions."

I have learned to unload my frustrations by way of a prayer, pouring out to God exactly what I feel and asking Him for wisdom, understanding and restraint to not act out of emotion. I write out some of my prayers in my journal because I have found that it helps me to focus my prayers, be more deliberate and ramble less. I also am better able to keep track of the answers to my journaled prayers. I don't journal some of my prayers, either because they are too personal in nature or too involved for my hand to keep up. Spiritual journaling isn't a requirement for maturity in Christ, nor the 11th Commandment, however it is a valuable tool to aid in spiritual maturity and a way of storing up blessings for the future.

We should expect opposition to our quiet time. We must be aware that enemies oppose the work of God and want to confound and confuse us. They will do whatever they can to keep us from spending time with God. We must do our part to protect the time we have set aside to spend with God by not allowing other things to creep in and rob us of our time, such as ringing phones, doorbells, or people. This is one reason why I encourage you to try early morning, before others are awake as the best time to meet with God. But remember that God loves to meet with us anytime day or night. He stands ready and waiting to enjoy our fellowship,

© Belonging to Him Ministries 2009. All rights reserved.

Sitting in Isaiah

minister to us and hear our prayers.

Having said all of that, I return to what I first said, that God wants our time with Him to be a blessing not a burden. So if you miss a day or two don't shame yourself or beat yourself up. Just return to Him for refreshment and enjoyment, understanding that He is your Abba (daddy) Father. He loves and enjoys your company and is ready, able and willing to lead you to be the person He created you to be.

Overview of the Book of Isaiah

Isaiah is sometimes referred to as the Fifth Gospel because its theme is very similar to that of the four Gospels telling of the coming of the Messiah, and of God's purpose and plan for salvation, as well as God's judgment of sin.

The name Isaiah means "Jehovah is salvation". Thus the key theme of Isaiah is the salvation—*deliverance* of the Lord. The key verse of the book is in Chapter 1:18 *"come now, let us reason together," says the Lord. "Though your sins are like scarlet, they shall be as white as snow, though they are red as crimson, they shall be like wool."* Isaiah, the son of Amoz was called to his ministry "in the year that King Uzziah died" (6:1) in 739B.C. Isaiah's ministry spanned 50 years and four kings. He was married and his wife was called a "prophetess" either because she herself had the gift of prophecy or because she was married to a prophet. Isaiah was a man who literally saw God and lived to tell about his experience. He was a man tuned into the Spirit of God who loved his country. Some call him a true patriot because he was not afraid to denounce Kings and priests in the name of God while warning the nation of Judah to turn back to God.

The nation of Israel had divided after the death of Solomon (1 Kings 20). The ten northern tribes became the Kingdom of Israel (Ephraim), with Samaria as its capitol city. "The two remaining tribes Benjamin and Judah united to form the kingdom of Judah, with Jerusalem as its capital city" (Weirsbe, p.11). Israel fell to Assyria in 722B.C. just as Isaiah had predicted would happen, but his main focus was on Judah and Jerusalem. His message to Judah remained clear that God would punish their sins of apostasy and idolatry and he predicted in Isaiah 6:9-12 that Judah would fail to turn back to God. In deed they did and they were nearly destroyed.

The book of Isaiah breaks naturally into two sections. Chapters 1-39 have a general theme of God's approaching judgment on the nation of Judah. "In some of the most striking passages in the Bible, the prophet announces that God will punish His people because of their sin, rebellion and worship of false gods. But this message of stern judgment is also mixed with beautiful poems of comfort and promise. Although judgment is surely coming, better days for God's Covenant People lie just ahead. This section of Isaiah's book refers several times to the coming MESSIAH. His name will be called IMMANUEL (7:14). As a ruler on the throne of David, he will establish an everlasting kingdom (9:7)." (Lockyer et al.)

"The second major section of Isaiah's book chapters 40-66 are filled with prophecies of comfort for the nation of Judah. Just as Isaiah warned of God's approaching judgment in the first part of his book, the 27 concluding chapters were written to comfort God's people in the midst of

Sitting in Isaiah

their suffering after His judgment had fallen. The theme of this entire section may be illustrated with Isaiah's famous hymn of comfort that God directed the prophet to address to the people: "Comfort, yes, comfort My people! says your God. Speak comfort to Jerusalem, and cry out to her, that her warfare is ended, that her iniquity is pardoned; for she has received from the Lord's hand double for all her sins" (40:1-2). (Lockyer et al.)

The Hebrew word for "comfort" also means "to repent". It's important for us to understand going forward that God gives comfort to repented souls, not to rebellious ones. The more we live in rebellion to God, the more we wound ourselves and in that depth of wounding we will indeed be in need of even more comfort. My exhortation to live free and clean will be woven throughout the study as I urge us to live clean lives for His glory and our own good.

Throughout the book Isaiah uses the phrase "the day of the Lord" which speaks of that future time when the whole world will taste God's judgment in a day of wrath upon the world, but his most immediate theme is the time in which we are living right now. Jesus the Messiah came as Isaiah prophesied he would. He died, rose again and now sits at the right hand of God the father to intercede on behalf of you and me. What an extraordinary day we live in. Do you think Isaiah watches us in amazement because we have so much yet live like we have so little?

Sitting in the spiritual spa of Isaiah, we will take an in-depth look at what brings devastation to our souls, and learn the path to recovery. We'll examine the potent toxins that pollute our souls along with how to be cleansed and get ourselves back to good spiritual health. After these treatments we'll also learn how to protect ourselves so that we can re-emerge from the spa to live refreshed, renewed and restored lives in God's presence.

And look for God to show up. He says, "I'll take the hand of those who don't know the way, who can't see where they're going. I'll be a personal guide to them, directing them . . . I'll be right there . . . These are the things I'll be doing for them – sticking with them, not leaving them for a minute" (Isaiah 42:16, THE MESSAGE).

© Belonging to Him Ministries 2009. All rights reserved.

Sitting in Isaiah

Chapter One

Isaiah 61

Sitting in Isaiah

Isaiah 61

The Spirit of the Sovereign LORD is on me, because the LORD has anointed me to preach good news to the poor. He has sent me to bind up the brokenhearted, to proclaim freedom for the captives and release from darkness for the prisoners, 2 to proclaim the year of the LORD's favor and the day of vengeance of our God, to comfort all who mourn, 3 and provide for those who grieve in Zion--to bestow on them a crown of beauty instead of ashes, the oil of gladness instead of mourning, and a garment of praise instead of a spirit of despair. They will be called oaks of righteousness, a planting of the LORD for the display of his splendor. 4 They will rebuild the ancient ruins and restore the places long devastated; they will renew the ruined cities that have been devastated for generations. 5 Aliens will shepherd your flocks; foreigners will work your fields and vineyards. 6 And you will be called priests of the LORD, you will be named ministers of our God. You will feed on the wealth of nations, and in their riches you will boast. 7 Instead of their shame my people will receive a double portion, and instead of disgrace they will rejoice in their inheritance; and so they will inherit a double portion in their land, and everlasting joy will be theirs. 8 "For I, the LORD, love justice; I hate robbery and iniquity. In my faithfulness I will reward them and make an everlasting covenant with them. 9 Their descendants will be known among the nations and their offspring among the peoples. All who see them will acknowledge that they are a people the LORD has blessed." 10 I delight greatly in the LORD; my soul rejoices in my God. For he has clothed me with garments of salvation and arrayed me in a robe of righteousness, as a bridegroom adorns his head like a priest, and as a bride adorns herself with her jewels. 11 For as the soil makes the sprout come up and a garden causes seeds to grow, so the Sovereign LORD will make righteousness and praise spring up before all nations.

(NIV)

Sitting in Isaiah

Chapter One   **Lesson One**

Read Isaiah 61. Key Verse: Isaiah 61:4 - "They will rebuild the ancient ruins and restore the places long devastated; they will renew the ruined cities that have been devastated for generations." **Review** this week's key verse and write it on an index card to carry with you to review throughout the day.

Isaiah 61:2 proclaims "the year of the Lord's favor" and refers to the *Year of Jubilee* described in Leviticus 25. Levitical law observed a sabbatical year every seventh year allowing the land to rest. After seven sabbaticals or 49 years they would celebrate the fiftieth year as the Year of Jubilee. During that year all accumulated debts were cancelled, all lands were returned to their original owners, all slaves were freed and everyone got a fresh new start in life! Imagine what life would be like for you if you were given a brand new start, a fresh new beginning, or a "do-over"? What might you do differently? In which areas of your life would you like a second chance? What new beginnings do you long for in your life?

It's so easy for our souls and spirits to grow tired, run down, fall into disrepair and be devastated just like the cities of Israel had. Whether it's a city or a soul, desolation, ruination, devastation and dilapidation occur either through neglect, drought, storms, abandonment or catastrophic events. Isaiah 61 refers to the abandoned cities and towns that had fallen in disrepair over time after Judah abandoned them. They were in desperate need of renovation and restoration. But figuratively speaking the message from Isaiah 61 also applies to us, our souls and our lives. Isaiah clearly communicates to us that God is the master renovator. He is the God of renewal and he is in the business of extreme makeovers of the spiritual kind!

In the book of Isaiah we find six factors that caused Judah's dwellings, cities and lives to fall into ruination and devastation. They were sin, oppression, loss, strongholds (such as idol worship), disappointment with God and people. In the coming chapters we will explore these six factors that also bring about devastation to our lives and we will see how these same factors can pollute, congest, infest and bring ruination to our souls.

© Belonging to Him Ministries 2009. All rights reserved.

Sitting in Isaiah

Our key verse for this chapter brings great hope to those of us living with generations of devastation. God can restore and renew devastated places of our lives, even those parts that have been in drought and decay for years. Some of us have aging foundations that are vulnerable and impotent from decay. From our key verse *ancient ruins* refers to areas so utterly destroyed that we have lost hope in believing they could ever be restored. *Ruined cities* represent multiple dwellings. Consider these multiple dwellings as multiple "woundings". Many of us carry wounds tucked away deep inside, and over time these wounds can turn our souls to ashes. These ruined cities inside us can result from rejection, loss, disappointments, sin, illnesses, or neglect, and in the absence of complete healing they accumulate inside us over time. Often they aren't from just one event, but a series of painful events, and either we haven't known how or haven't taken the time to heal from them. These wounds are very present in us despite our efforts to deny their existence. Others can usually see their effects in us. Our wounds need our attention.

Can you recall a time in your life when you felt devastated over something that happened to you? What difficulties have you faced that have been hard for you to bounce back from? Are there any ancient ruins, dilapidated dwellings or devastated places? Is there anything in your life threatening to overtake you?

Take some time to reflect on the questions above and answer one or two of them in the space below.

Isaiah 58:12 states that God's people would be known as the *"people who will rebuild the ancient ruins and will raise up the age-old foundations; you will be called Repairer of Broken Walls, Restorer of Streets with Dwellings"*. Who does the work to rebuild? What will be rebuilt and what will the workers be called?

© Belonging to Him Ministries 2009. All rights reserved.

Sitting in Isaiah

Often I wish God would renovate my soul the way they renovate people's homes on the TV show *Extreme Makeover: Home Edition*! I would love to check out and go on vacation while He renovates my soul and then return home to find it all changed and brand new! But He doesn't! He doesn't sweep us away on a luxury vacation while he renovates the devastated places of our lives, bringing us home in style for a grand entrance into a new life! God involves us in the work of rebuilding our lives! God tells us to get on our work clothes and get to work. He supplies everything we need to do the job; knowledge, strength, endurance, protection, comfort, provision, wisdom, materials, counsel and support. He gives us a blueprint for renovation, and a crew to help out. But the work is ours to do.

Spend a few minutes reflecting on the truth of Isaiah 61. Write a prayer below asking God to meet you right where you are today. Ask Him for his presence and power to be poured out into your soul. Seek Him for grace as you allow Him to begin your soul makeover in the Spiritual Spa.

Optional reading assignment for today: Isaiah Chapter 2.

© Belonging to Him Ministries 2009. All rights reserved.

Sitting in Isaiah

Chapter One   **Lesson Two**

Read Isaiah 61 in your favorite translation. **Review** this week's key verse Isaiah 61:4. **Re-read** today's focus verses 61:1-3, and write down what the seven "good news" is that Isaiah has been sent to preach in verses 1-3. According to these verses what does it mean to you to be saved by Jesus?

In verse 1 Isaiah describes two types of prisoners, those who are held captive and those who are bound in darkness.

Recently two female American journalists held in captivity in North Korea were set free. Memories of their tears of joy as they were released overwhelms me, even now. But can you imagine the scene if these women had refused their freedom, even after President Clinton had negotiated their release and was standing right in front of them ready to take them home? What if they had told Mr. Clinton, "Thanks Sir, but no thanks. We like our prison and prefer to stay here"?

Everyone has to fight to get out and remain free from captivity. Satan loves bondage and he is an expert at holding us captive and imprisoned. Isaiah 61 lists some of the things that hold many of us in captivity. As you take a second look at Isaiah 61 today, write down those things that hold us captive. Hint: the first one listed is poverty in verse 1.

© Belonging to Him Ministries 2009. All rights reserved.

Sitting in Isaiah

Some of us live at risk of captivity because we are by nature pit dwellers and though we might not want to admit it, we love the "activity of captivity". Pit dwellers either jump, slip or allow themselves to get thrown into a dungeon. In her book *Get Out Of That Pit,* Beth Moore refers to pit dwelling as "a shadowy home of the heart, mind and soul so close and personal that, like mud on a set of tires, we drag it along wherever our physical circumstances move us". Beth describes three ways you know you are in a pit: 1) you feel stuck, 2) you can't stand up, and 3) you've lost vision (Moore, *Get Out of That Pit*, pp. 14-17).

Though it sounds absurd that anyone would prefer being held captive by anything or to be a dungeon dweller rather than know complete and total freedom, tragically some of us live that way every day. Daily Jesus stands before us, ready, willing and especially able to set us free from whatever is holding us captive, but we refuse Him. Each day we have a choice to make - to be free…..or not.

What is holding you captive today? Is it food, love of money, worship of idols, covetousness, un-forgiveness, bitterness, pain, poverty, illness, loss, feelings of rejection, anxiety, shame, loneliness, depression, insecurity, low self-esteem, or something else? Take a few moments to reflect upon today's lesson and write out truths found in Isaiah 61 that you need to take to your heart and apply.

Optional reading assignment for today: Isaiah Chapter 3.

© Belonging to Him Ministries 2009. All rights reserved.

Sitting in Isaiah

Chapter One   **Lesson Three**

Read all of Isaiah 61 out loud. **Review** this week's key verse Isaiah 61:4 by saying it out loud. **Re-read** today's focus verses Isaiah 61:2-3. The symbol of ashes rubbed onto the body to identify one with mourning is seen throughout the Old Testament (Esther 4 and 2 Samuel 13). Psalm 102:9 talks of eating ashes to express the deepest misery and degradation of the soul.

What does God promise for those who are in grief according to verse 3? What were they mourning over in Zion (verse 2)?

Zion refers to the promised land of Israel, where God would come and dwell with His chosen people. Those who were mourning in Zion at this time were a discouraged nation of Jewish exiles who were returning to a devastated impoverished land and a ruined temple. The Israelites and their ancestors had lost the land that God had given them and been taken away to Babylon because of their rebellion and disobedience to God! As they made their way home they were confronted by devastation in their cities, towns and villages.

Often the consequences of our sin bring great loss and grief to our lives. The consequences of sin are of a greater magnitude than you or I might be able to comprehend here on earth because sin brings incredible loss to God. Sin brings death and it ruins and destroys everything it touches. When we finally break free from being held captive by our sins, turn and come back home to God, we still face the results and natural consequences of our sin.

Have you ever returned to the Lord after a time of living in disobedience to God only to discover your life in need of major repair work? Have you experienced the pain of living with the natural consequences to your sin? Reflect and journal your experience below.

© Belonging to Him Ministries 2009. All rights reserved.

Sitting in Isaiah

Isaiah 61 confirms to us that God is really good at giving His people a makeover of the spiritual kind! Yes, a spiritual makeover! Ever noticed how hard it is to watch someone who is in turmoil and grief? Their face is often contorted by pain. God wants to give you a new look and put a new face on you even though you may be in pain and grief! He begins by giving you beauty instead of ashes. The Hebrew word translated as *beauty* is pe'er (peh-ayr'), which means an embellishment on the head or a beautiful headdress. I like to picture a tiara or a crown.

The second part of God's makeover from Isaiah 61 is the *oil of gladness* which literally means the "grease of joy". Most women don't like shine on their faces, but that is exactly what this means! God wants our faces to shine with joy even when we are sad. Sound impossible? It's not. Joy is not the same as happiness. Happiness is more of a circumstantial joy, like a mood that comes and goes. Real joy is an attribute of the Spirit of God (Gal. 5:22). Joy comes to us from being in the presence of God just like it came to Moses in Exodus 34:29. Moses had been on the mountain in the presence of God and when he returned to the people in the valley, his face was radiant! We get filled with joy by being filled up with God.

I have a precious friend fighting terminal cancer. She has suffered many losses in her life the past few years—not only her health, but her career and her home. If anyone had a reason to be sad it should be her. She may be sad some days, but she is never without joy. Her face shines with the joy of the Lord. She has peace and knows contentment even when life around her seems to be falling down. How? She sits in the presence of the almighty God and allows Him to fill her with His joy.

The beauty and oil of joy God offers to those of us who are in mourning is not to prevent us from mourning but to give us hope while we mourn. Grieving out our losses is healthy and a natural part of life. God is promising to give you comfort when you mourn so that you will have hope and not fall into a spirit of despair. What are some of the losses you have suffered that have been particularly difficult for you to bear? Reflect on today's truth and write a prayer asking God to help you apply truth so that you can find His crown of beauty for you and His oil of gladness.

Optional reading assignment for today: Isaiah Chapter 4.

Sitting in Isaiah

Chapter One   **Lesson Four**

Read all of Isaiah 61 and notice what God promises. **Review** this week's key verse Isaiah 61:4 without looking, from memory. **Re-read** today's focus verses Isaiah 61:3-7, and consider what it means to wear a garment of praise in stead of a spirit of despair. Praise means *a hymn* to show admiration. It is from the Hebrew root word *halal (haw-lal')*, which literally means to shine, to make a show, to boast; and thus to be loudly foolish; to rave; to purposefully celebrate.

Have you or someone you know ever been without hope and felt despair? What do you think Isaiah means by *a garment of praise instead of a spirit of despair*?

It is normal to be tempted to feel despair when we are faced with the wreckage and waste of devastation in our life and our soul. Despair is a normal human reaction to desolation but it isn't the right reaction, in fact it is a sin to allow ourselves to sink into a pit of despair.

To despair is to have a profound feeling that there is no hope, that all is lost. Loss of hope is a major factor in desolation of the soul. Judah based their hope of what they saw with their physical eyes. They based their hope on their circumstances. Their loss of hope in God caused them to make very unwise and ungodly decisions that impacted their nation's history for generations to come.

When we allow ourselves to sink into a pit of despair and hopelessness we are giving in to the enemy. To be without hope means we don't believe God is who He says He is and will do what He says He will do. The Israelites were living in a time when God was very silent toward them. In years past God had done many signs and miracles for them like producing water from a rock in the desert and appearing before them in clouds and fire.

Have you ever had a time in your life when you felt God was far from you, even silent with you? How did you handle that period of time with God? Recall if you can, what happened to break the distance between you and God.

© Belonging to Him Ministries 2009. All rights reserved.

Sitting in Isaiah

A spirit of despair is from the enemy and to allow ourselves to fall into the trap of discouragement and despair is to award Satan a victory in our lives. Satan wants nothing more than for us to know complete and utter despair, because in despair our focus is not on God but on ourselves and our circumstances! But with God we are never without hope. We may be *hard pressed on every side, but not crushed; perplexed, but not in despair; persecuted, but not abandoned, struck down, but not destroyed"*. 2 Corinthians 4:8

Is your hope in God waning, decreasing and lessening? What specifically happened to bring you to a place of discouragement?

We find hope in God when we praise Him. If circumstances around us seem to be spinning out of control, and we feel panic and despair stirring up inside of us it is time to put on our garments of praise.

Write a prayer of praise to Him in the space provided below. Ask Him to give you a spirit of praise and to increase your faith in Him. Praise Him by expressing your love for Him, thanking Him for who He is and recall some things that He has done, either for you or for others. Use 2 Corinthians 4:8 as a prayer for God to strengthen and encourage you.

Optional reading assignment for today: Isaiah Chapter 6.

© Belonging to Him Ministries 2009. All rights reserved.

Sitting in Isaiah

Chapter One   **Lesson Five**

Read all of Isaiah 61 as a prayer. **Review** this week's key verse Isaiah 61:4 by writing it from memory. **Re-read** today's focus verses 10-11 and notice the spiritual clothing and accessories we are promised. Make a list below. What is the standard of quality that Jesus will use to clothe and accessorize us? Hint: see the phrase "as a" for your answer. What is the significance of our spiritual clothing and accessories?

The Hebrew word translated clothed is *labash* (law-bash') and means to wrap around, to put on a garment or clothe oneself or another. Robe in this passage refers to a covering; an upper and outer garment. The word adorn is to put on regalia. Regalia are the ensigns or emblems or decorations of royalty like a crown or scepter. Adorn is similar to decking; to bring an ornament upon, and jewels are any apparatus that accessorizes the recipient.

Genesis 3:21 is the first time in the Bible that we see the use of the word *labash*. "The LORD God made garments of skin for Adam and his wife and *clothed* (*labash*) them". This is one of the tenderest moments in all the Bible as we watch God's sensitive compassionate heart in action. He was so terribly saddened and disappointed (though not surprised) by Adam and Eve's disobedience, yet still so full of tender compassion for them that He actually *made* them clothing before they left the Garden of Eden. The word *made* is the same word from Genesis 1:6 when God *made* the sky. What a touching scene of God's tender loving care to provide for them before they left the protection of the Garden.

I especially love the idea of God clothing us because I just wouldn't enjoy being naked in public! In truth, the thought of being naked is what turns me off to the idea of going to a spa. I'm just too self-conscious to enjoy "spa-ing". But in God's spiritual spa He asks us to bare our

© Belonging to Him Ministries 2009. All rights reserved.

Sitting in Isaiah

souls and come spiritually naked before Him. We can't wear our spiritual *Spanx* before God (those popular girdles that make us look really good in our clothing). God sees right through such facades.

Before we can wear God's garments of salvation and righteousness along with the accessories that magnify His glory in us, we must first strip down our souls for Him. First we must get vulnerable, open and honest before God. We must be who we really are so that God can then make us into who He meant for us to be.

Who are you, really? What are your deepest struggles that you are afraid to talk to God about? You know that He already knows who you are and your struggles. Write a prayer expressing to God your insecurities, doubts, failures, dreams and desires.

Our honesty and vulnerability with God is what moves His heart of compassion toward us. Just as the prodigal son found prodigal love when he returned home in honest humility before his father, so we can know that kind of love and acceptance for who we are right now at this moment. Oh my beloved, do you see how precious you are to Him and what He wants to do for you?

> *"But the father said to his servants, 'Quick! Bring the best robe and put it on him. Put a ring on his finger and sandals on his feet. Bring the fattened calf and kill it. Let's have a feast and celebrate. For this son of mine was dead and is alive again; he was lost and is found.' So they began to celebrate".* (Luke 15:22-24)

How much time do you spend worrying about how you look (physically)? Be honest. How does that time spent compare to time spent throughout your day meditating on God's word, listening to His voice, being obedient and concerned for your relationship with Him? Do you ask Him to show you "what not to wear" (and I'm not referring to physical clothing, but the spiritual kind)?

© Belonging to Him Ministries 2009. All rights reserved.

Sitting in Isaiah

Admitting our need for a savior from our sins and accepting Jesus as Savior allows us to wear the garments of salvation which are a covering for our souls. The garments of salvation are very expensive indeed for they were paid for with the blood of Jesus. By accepting Jesus as our Savior we are assigned or accredited with the righteousness of Christ, so that God sees us as holy and pure through the righteousness of Jesus.

If you have never asked Jesus to be your Savior, write a prayer below admitting your sin and your needs, asking Him into your heart and your life. If you are in Christ, write a prayer thanking Him for your "soul-wear" and your salvation. Thank Him for the difference He has made in your life. Mention to Him those you may know who need to know Him, asking Him to lead them to salvation.

Optional reading assignment for today: Isaiah Chapter 7.

© Belonging to Him Ministries 2009. All rights reserved.

Chapter Two

Isaiah 1

Sitting in Isaiah

Isaiah 1

The vision concerning Judah and Jerusalem that Isaiah son of Amoz saw during the reigns of Uzziah, Jotham, Ahaz and Hezekiah, kings of Judah. [2] Hear, O heavens! Listen, O earth! For the LORD has spoken: "I reared children and brought them up, but they have rebelled against me. [3] The ox knows his master, the donkey his owner's manger, but Israel does not know, my people do not understand." [4] Ah, sinful nation, a people loaded with guilt, a brood of evildoers, children given to corruption! They have forsaken the LORD; they have spurned the Holy One of Israel and turned their backs on him. [5] Why should you be beaten anymore? Why do you persist in rebellion? Your whole head is injured, your whole heart afflicted. [6] From the sole of your foot to the top of your head there is no soundness--only wounds and welts and open sores, not cleansed or bandaged or soothed with oil. [7] Your country is desolate, our cities burned with fire; your fields are being stripped by foreigners right before you, laid waste as when overthrown by strangers. [8] The Daughter of Zion is left like a shelter in a vineyard, like a hut in a field of melons, like a city under siege. [9] Unless the LORD Almighty had left us some survivors, we would have become like Sodom, we would have been like Gomorrah. [10] Hear the word of the LORD, you rulers of Sodom; listen to the law of our God, you people of Gomorrah! [11] "The multitude of your sacrifices-- what are they to me?" says the LORD."I have more than enough of burnt offerings, of rams and the fat of fattened animals; I have no pleasure in the blood of bulls and lambs and goats. [12] When you come to appear before me, who has asked this of you, this trampling of my courts? [13] Stop bringing meaningless offerings! Your incense is detestable to me. New Moons, Sabbaths and convocations--I cannot bear your evil assemblies. [14] Your New Moon festivals and your appointed feasts my soul hates. They have become a burden to me; I am weary of bearing them. [15] When you spread out your hands in prayer, I will hide my eyes from you; even if you offer many prayers, I will not listen. Your hands are full of blood; [16] wash and make yourselves clean. Take your evil deeds out of my sight! Stop doing wrong, [17] learn to do right! Seek justice, encourage the oppressed. Defend the cause of the fatherless, plead the case of the widow. [18] "Come now, let us reason together," says the LORD. "Though your sins are like scarlet they shall be as white as snow; though they are red as crimson, they shall be like wool. [19] If you are willing and obedient, you will eat the best from the land; [20] but if you resist and rebel, you will be devoured by the sword." For the mouth of the LORD has spoken. [21] See how the faithful city has become a harlot! She once was full of justice; righteousness used to dwell in her--but now murderers! [22] Your silver has become dross, your choice wine is diluted with water. [23] Your rulers are rebels, companions of thieves; they all love bribes and chase after gifts. They do not defend the cause of the fatherless; the widow's case does not come before them. [24] Therefore the Lord, the LORD Almighty, the Mighty One of Israel, declares: "Ah, I will get relief from my foes and avenge myself on my enemies. [25] I will turn my hand against you; I will thoroughly purge away your dross and remove all your impurities. [26] I will restore your judges as in days of old, your counselors as at the beginning. Afterward you will be called the City of Righteousness, the Faithful City." [27] Zion will be redeemed with justice, her penitent ones with righteousness. [28] But rebels and sinners will both be broken, and those who forsake the LORD will perish. [29] "You will be ashamed because of the sacred oaks in which you have delighted; you will be disgraced because of the gardens that you have chosen. [30] You will be like an oak with fading leaves, like a garden without water. [31] The mighty man will become tinder and his work a spark; both will burn together, with no one to quench the fire."

(NIV)

© Belonging to Him Ministries 2009. All rights reserved.

Sitting in Isaiah

Chapter Two **Lesson One**

Read Isaiah 1. **Key Verse** Isaiah 1:18 "Come now, let us reason together," says the LORD. "Though your sins are like scarlet they shall be as white as snow; though they are red as crimson, they shall be like wool". **Review** this week's key verse and write it on an index card to carry with you to review throughout the day.

Isaiah 1 opens with a vision Isaiah had from God concerning Judah and Jerusalem. Isaiah denounces sin both personal and national. It's as if he is giving us a "before" picture of what happens to us when we are left to ourselves. As the book of Isaiah goes on we will see more and more of the "after" picture of what God promises to do for all those he saves (Ortlund, p. 26). From our key verse this week the word translated *reason* means to decide a case in court. Instead of God pronouncing judgment on us, he offers us mercy and a pardon. We receive complete forgiveness for our sins. What is your definition of sin and why do you think it is such a big deal to God? From the key verse what is significant about the colors of sin and forgiveness, and what do these colors represent to you?

To sin is to do *anything* that is contrary to the character of God. Sin is either committed willfully and knowingly in open rebellion to God and his character, or it may be out of our own ignorance, because we just aren't aware that what we are doing or *not doing* is sinful. But all sin separates us from God. God hates sin, all sin, but He allows sin to reign for now so that we can be free to choose to live for Him, or not. Both sin and Satan have a limited time here on the earth (Revelation 20).

I have discovered, as Isaiah had in his day that it is not fun, popular or fashionable to talk about sin, but we must. Our spiritual spa treatment in Isaiah will not be spiritually rejuvenating unless we look at the issue of sin, because sin is what devastates and ruins our soul. Sin is what ruined the nation of Israel. Isaiah 1 gives a poignant picture of the effect sin has on us. Write a list of the effects of sin from Isaiah 1:5-6.

© Belonging to Him Ministries 2009. All rights reserved.

Sitting in Isaiah

The world's philosophy teaches that having an awareness of sin is damaging to one's psyche. Actually the opposite is true. Not having a sense of sin is very damaging to our entire being! Having a sense of sin is life giving, not self-destructive. We hear so much about the need to build self-esteem, and it is important to have proper self-esteem. But the central key element to a truly healthy self-esteem is seeing your self humbly through God's eyes. We need to begin in humility (but not by beating ourself up—that's false humility), and then accept the fact that we are sinners who need to be saved from ourselves. On the surface, not discussing or examining our sin may seem like good self-esteem management, but the reality is that when we ignore or deny our sin we are choosing to stay in prison. When we get honest with God and others about our sin we experience freedom because we can stop pretending to be someone we are not (John 8:31-32)!

In verse 5 Isaiah refers to being beaten. Does he mean that God is beating them or are they beating themselves with their own sin? In what ways have you seen the wounding effects of sin on your life?

What does it mean to you that God offers you a complete pardon for your sin? Write a prayer thanking God for His complete forgiveness and ask Him to help you accept His forgiveness and move forward from here.

Optional reading assignment for today: Isaiah Chapter 8.

© Belonging to Him Ministries 2009. All rights reserved.

Sitting in Isaiah

Chapter Two **Lesson Two**

Read Isaiah One and look for the sins which the Israelites had been committing. **Review** this week's key verse Isaiah 1:18. **Read** today's focus verses 1-7. In verse 3 God says that there is something they/we don't know and understand. What is it? Isaiah describes Judah's sins in 1:1-7. List them below.

Walking the road of obedience can be challenging. The world around us tries hard to convince us that obedience is boring. If we are being honest (and we certainly need to be) then we would confess that some sin seems fun, at least for a moment. If there weren't something fun or appealing about sin, then why would we bother with it? God doesn't require us to a live a perfect life, but He does call us to repentance. Look back over verses 1-7 of Isaiah 1 again. Judah was guilty of a deeper core sin, what do you think it might have been?

It's easy to look only at our surface-level behavioral sins like lying, stealing, coveting, addictions and adultery, but what we really need to do is dig down into the roots of our choices and behaviors. All sin is sin, but some surface-level sins are actually symptomatic of a deeper sin, *the sin of despising God*. Ray Ortlund explains:

© Belonging to Him Ministries 2009. All rights reserved.

Sitting in Isaiah

"To forsake the Lord is to treat him as the last resort rather than as the fountainhead. To despise God is to disrelish him, to put a discount on God while valuing other things. And that condition of the heart estranges us from God because of who God is." (Ortlund, p. 29)

It is very common in the church to be among those who despise the Lord God and perhaps don't even realize it because they are practicing good religion, going to church, praying, reading the Bible and serving God all while discounting and devaluing Him. We are plagued with the disease of self-devaluation - we underestimate how deeply God values us and how much our devaluation of Him grieves Him as it widens the gulf between us and Him.

In what ways have you been devaluing or perhaps even despising God without realizing it? If you realize that you haven't been honoring and valuing God as you should, write a prayer of confession. Reflect on some tangible ways that you can demonstrate (with His help) how much you personally value Him and write a prayer of commitment to follow through on those ideas. If you aren't sure, ask Him to reveal the answers to you. Use the space below to record your prayers.

Since we are forgiven of all our sin at the time of salvation, why do you think we need to be so concerned about confessing what we might consider to be our "little sins" day to day? Why do we need to be specific with God about our mistakes and not generalize?

© Belonging to Him Ministries 2009. All rights reserved.

Sitting in Isaiah

Read Isaiah 1:5-6 thoughtfully, and journal a prayer to God asking Him to reveal the sin in your life that is wounding you—leaving your soul with welts and open sores from the sole of your feet to the top of your head. Wait in silence before Him allowing Him time to move, reveal and speak to you. Record what you hear Him telling you. As He reveals truth to you, ask Him to cleanse you. Finish with a prayer of commitment to live a clean life that is pleasing to Him in every way and to heighten your awareness to sin.

Optional reading assignment for today: Isaiah Chapter 9.

Sitting in Isaiah

Chapter Two **Lesson Three**

Read all of Isaiah 1 in your favorite translation. **Review** this week's key verse Isaiah 1:18 by saying it out loud. As you read today's focus verses 10-20, see what God says He had more than enough of in verse 11. What do you think God wants from us according to these verses?

Isaiah was an upfront, in–your-face kind of guy. In verses 9 and 10 Isaiah compared the Israelites to the people of Sodom and Gomorrah, two cities so evil that they were destroyed after many merciful attempts to save them failed to bring them to repentance (Genesis 13-19). Most certainly the Israelites felt it was audacious of Isaiah to compare them to Sodom and Gomorrah, suggesting that they deserved God's fiery judgment because they suffered with the sin of hypocrisy.

A hypocrite pretends to be something they are not. The word only occurs once in the Old Testament in Isaiah 32:6 and is translated *ungodliness* in most English language Bibles. It means to cover or hide; to *pollute or* defile; and to seduce. The word is used often in the New Testament and in Greek reflects one who acts in a play or drama wearing a mask and playing a part . . . pretending (Matthew 6:1-2, 5, 16; Luke 20:19-20; James 3:17).

What God found so offensive in the Israelites was not what they were doing as much as what they were *not* doing. They were not making repentance part of their worship. The difference between someone who is pretending and someone who's not a hypocrite is *authenticity*. To be authentic is to be genuine or real. God seeks genuine repentance from us. He isn't as concerned about our sacrifices, offerings, good deeds and worship as much as He is concerned about the condition of our hearts. God is all about authenticity and He abhors hypocrisy. He doesn't want us pretending to be someone we aren't. He doesn't expect us to be perfect, but He does expect us to be real about the sin in our lives. Being authentic people means being repentant humble people.

© Belonging to Him Ministries 2009. All rights reserved.

Sitting in Isaiah

Over time pretending with God and others brings drought and barrenness to our souls. An unrepentant soul is toxic and devastated, because a haughty (proud) spirit will be separated from God and His healing. I'm not talking about eternal separation but about fellowship. James 4:6 says that "God is opposed to the proud but gives grace to the humble." If you are living a life of un-confessed sin that you are afraid to deal with before God because you don't want to look at your sin, or because you don't want to change, then you have set your soul on a course for complete ruin.

In what ways might you be pretending rather than being real? Take a few minutes to reflect on your relationship with God and others. Ask Him to reveal truth about your inner self, and things that perhaps up until now you weren't aware of. Psalm 51:6 says, *"Surely you desire truth in the inner parts; you teach me wisdom in the inmost place"*.

Ray Ortlund helps us understand true repentance in his book *God Saves Sinners:*

> "True repentance makes things right again. All that keeps us from renewal with God is our own stubbornness. It isn't as though the path forward is a mystery or hard to find. God is only asking us to be open and responsive. The only conviction of sin that ends up healing us is when we see how we have despised and forsaken the very one who died to save us. Repentance of that super-sin opens up healing for all of our other sins." (p. 31)

Psalm 139:23-24 says, "Search me, O God, and know my heart; test me and know my anxious thoughts. See if there is any offensive way in me, and lead me in the way everlasting".

1 John 1:9-10 says, "If we confess our sins, he is faithful and just and will forgive us our sins and purify us from all unrighteousness. If we claim we have not sinned, we make him out to be a liar and his word has no place in our lives."

Write a prayer asking God to move in the hearts of those in your life who are in need of God's free gift of salvation or perhaps a re-commitment to Him. Journal any other concerns you may have in the space provided below.

© Belonging to Him Ministries 2009. All rights reserved.

Sitting in Isaiah

Optional reading assignment for today: Isaiah Chapter 10.

© Belonging to Him Ministries 2009. All rights reserved.

Sitting in Isaiah

Chapter Two   **Lesson Four**

Read all of Isaiah 1 out loud. **Review** this week's key verse Isaiah 1:18 without looking, from memory. **Re-read** today's focus verses 17-23 and notice the word "oppressed" in verse 17 which comes from the Hebrew word *chamowts* (khaw-motse') which means violated, with the implication of being robbed. *Oppress* means to dominate harshly, inflect stress upon, to exercise power over, to harass. Can you recall a time when you felt oppressed? What were you going through and how did you feel?

Living under oppression can inflict devastating wounds to our souls. Oppression can leave our souls desolate, devastated and ruined . . . *if we allow it to*. All oppression is evil. Our oppressors never mean to do us good as they inflict their evil against us (Genesis 50:20). We can experience oppression two ways, from others or from Satan. Through the media and global communications we can see for ourselves the suffering and afflictions of many around the world vividly, any day of the week. The fact that God allows evil and suffering in the world is a problem for some of us and we wonder if God is so powerful, why doesn't He just wipe out all evil? What do you think about this? Write your answer below.

Satan was an angel named Lucifer that decided he might fare better by being God's enemy than God's friend. The moment he made that decision he was cast out of heaven and he took a host of angels (now demons) with him. God's eye is ever upon him and he isn't able to do anything without God's ultimate permission and approval (Isaiah 14:12-15; Ezekiel 28:11-19; Revelation 12). Satan has limited time, resources and power (Job 1:12; Luke 4:6; 2 Thessalonians 2:7-8) He is known as the "ruler of this world" and the "god of this age" and "the prince of the power of the air" (John 12:31; 2 Corinthians 4:4; Ephesians 2:2). Time is running out for Satan and his reign on earth. When Christ returns he and his demons will be thrown into the lake of fire

© Belonging to Him Ministries 2009. All rights reserved.

Sitting in Isaiah

(Revelation 20). As believers it is imperative that we focus on the truth that Jesus defeated Satan at the cross and in His resurrection. By faith we can live in this victory over Satan every day because we know that Jesus already has won the final battle.

Oppression is not the same as possession. If you have invited Jesus into your life as your savior then you belong to Him. Believers can't be possessed. Satan is a squatter and likes to hang around some times if *we let him.* Satan loves to use our sins or the sins of others to oppress us if we *let him.* Although we are forgiven of our sins, we will still bear the natural consequences of them. *We have authority over Satan if we are under the blood of Jesus. We are commanded to stand against him and do everything we must do to stand* (Ephesians 6). But proceed cautiously beloved. Don't glorify Satan by blaming everything that is going wrong in your life on him or by being afraid of him. Take responsibility before God if you have made some mistakes, get your focus on Jesus and His forgiveness, put on the armor everyday (Ephesians 6) and get back to doing and being what God has called you to be and do.

The following is a prayer from Joe Vigliano to follow when you are under oppression.

> Heavenly Father,
>
> I know from the work of Jesus Christ that Satan and his minions are a defeated enemy. I also know from Your Word that the enemy continues to roam the earth and attack us. LORD, I ask for Your help in putting on the armor — the helmet of salvation, the breastplate of righteousness, the shield of faith, the shoes of the gospel of peace, the belt of truth, and the sword of the Spirit (Your Word)--in order to resist the enemy so he will flee.
>
> By the authority of Jesus and in the power of His shed blood, I ask You to summon warrior angels to fight on my behalf if necessary. And if it is Your will for me to confront the evil spirits of the enemy directly, I ask You to guide me and protect me as I strive to pray and to live within Your will.
>
> Grant me the patience, Father, to know that deliverance from the enemy isn't always immediate. Grant me a resolute spirit so that I am persistent in my prayer and steadfast in my resistance. And grant me the wisdom to remain alert, especially when it seems as if the enemy has moved on and ended his attack on me.
>
> I praise You, Jesus, for Your victory over the enemy, for his complete defeat, and I claim that victory for myself as I abide in You.
>
> In Your Holy Name I pray, Jesus,
>
> Amen

© Belonging to Him Ministries 2009. All rights reserved.

Sitting in Isaiah

Optional reading assignment for today: Isaiah Chapter 11.

Sitting in Isaiah

Chapter Two **Lesson Five**

Read all of Isaiah 1. **Review** this week's key verse Isaiah 1:18 by writing it from memory. **Re-read** today's focus verses Isaiah 1:18-23. Read Mark 14:32-41 and notice how Jesus coped with oppression. Write your observations below.

When Jesus felt oppressed He would:
1) **Gather His trusted friends around him and avoid isolation**. Even though His friends had previously failed him by not staying awake to pray for Him, He included them anyway. Some of us have very high expectations of our friends, maybe too high. We are looking for perfection, and if we expect that friends might let us down, we just don't want to reach out and be disappointed…*again*. Often when we are oppressed either physically, emotionally or spiritually we withdraw from others. Sometimes we withdraw because we are afraid of rejection. We are embarrassed and ashamed or depressed and just don't want anyone around. Isolation leaves an open door for Satan. He works to isolate us by causing us to hide and not be honest about our oppressive condition because we fear rejection (this too is our pride at work). When we are under affliction we should seek to not be alone and reach out to someone whom we can trust in Christ.

Do you have trusted friends that you can turn to in your time of need? If so, write a prayer thanking God for them and then be sure to share your gratitude with your friends. If no, write a prayer pouring out your need before God and asking Him to supply those friends to you.

© Belonging to Him Ministries 2009. All rights reserved.

Sitting in Isaiah

2) **Go to a familiar place of prayer**. Do you have a place for prayer? It can be a special chair, or a "prayer room" in your car, a closet, a bathroom or a back porch, wherever you have a sense of God's presence. This will help you have a more meaningful prayer time. Regularly returning to a familiar place, hopefully at the same time of day aids us in having productive prayer time.

   Where is your place of prayer and how frequently do you visit it? What makes your prayer place special to you?

3) **Humble yourself before God**. It can help to kneel or lay face-down.

4) **Pray God's Word back to Him**. Jesus prayed back to His Father from the Scriptures that with God all things are possible. When oppression comes in the form of physical suffering, spiritual affliction or emotional storms, our emotional response will be strong. While our emotions are part of who we are, we should not allow how we feel to divert us from truth of God's Word. As believers our lives and actions are to be based in truth. Praying back God's Word to Him is powerful, and makes His Word come alive for us with power. Jesus didn't feel up to dying on a cross for us, but He knew and prayed back His Father's Word, and was filled with the power and strength to persist and obey.

5) **Be authentic with God**. Being real with God about how we really feel and what we really need is key to finding hope, help and healing.

6) **Ask**. Present your requests to God and find help in your time of need.

© Belonging to Him Ministries 2009. All rights reserved.

Sitting in Isaiah

7) **Submit**. Jesus had the power to step in and change his situation, but he didn't. He didn't try to control or fix the situation on his own but instead left the outcome of his fate in the hands of his Abba Father. He submitted himself to His father's will saying "not what I will, but what you will". Surrender to God is a key element in finding hope in oppression. Put your trust in God and recognize who He is: omniscient, omnipotent, Holy, just, righteous, loving, good, and that He has a plan for our good, not disaster (Jeremiah 29:11).

8) **Persist and endure** in prayer for as long as possible. We need to remain in prayer until our burden is lifted or until we find the strength we need. Prayer is work and takes energy, commitment, resolve and persistence.

Oh Beloved Friend, if you are suffering with oppression my heart breaks for you because I know your burden is heavy. Whether you brought the suffering on yourself through opening the door to sin, or whether it has been put upon you by another, you don't have to allow the enemy to keep your soul in a constant state of ruin and disrepair. God wants you to be lifted up, to know joy in the midst of your sorrow. God may not change your circumstances, as He didn't for Jesus in this passage. But God gave Him the strength to face His suffering, as He will for you too! How will you apply this lesson?

Optional reading assignment for today: Isaiah Chapter 12.

© Belonging to Him Ministries 2009. All rights reserved.

Chapter Three

Isaiah 40

Sitting in Isaiah

Isaiah 40

Comfort, comfort my people, says your God. [2] Speak tenderly to Jerusalem, and proclaim to her that her hard service has been completed, that her sin has been paid for, that she has received from the LORD's hand double for all her sins. [3] A voice of one calling: "In the desert prepare the way for the LORD; make straight in the wilderness a highway for our God. [4] Every valley shall be raised up, every mountain and hill made low; the rough ground shall become level, the rugged places a plain. [5] And the glory of the LORD will be revealed, and all mankind together will see it. For the mouth of the LORD has spoken." [6] A voice says, "Cry out. "And I said, "What shall I cry?" "All men are like grass, and all their glory is like the flowers of the field. [7] The grass withers and the flowers fall, because the breath of the LORD blows on them. Surely the people are grass. [8] The grass withers and the flowers fall, but the word of our God stands forever." [9] You who bring good tidings to Zion, go up on a high mountain. You who bring good tidings to Jerusalem, lift up your voice with a shout, lift it up, do not be afraid; say to the towns of Judah, "Here is your God!" [10] See, the Sovereign LORD comes with power, and his arm rules for him. See, his reward is with him, and his recompense accompanies him. [11] He tends his flock like a shepherd: He gathers the lambs in his arms and carries them close to his heart; he gently leads those that have young. [12] Who has measured the waters in the hollow of his hand, or with the breadth of his hand marked off the heavens? Who has held the dust of the earth in a basket, or weighed the mountains on the scales and the hills in a balance? [13] Who has understood the mind of the LORD, or instructed him as his counselor? [14] Whom did the LORD consult to enlighten him, and who taught him the right way? Who was it that taught him knowledge or showed him the path of understanding? [15] Surely the nations are like a drop in a bucket; they are regarded as dust on the scales; he weighs the islands as though they were fine dust. [16] Lebanon is not sufficient for altar fires, nor its animals enough for burnt offerings. [17] Before him all the nations are as nothing; they are regarded by him as worthless and less than nothing. [18] To whom, then, will you compare God? What image will you compare him to? [19] As for an idol, a craftsman casts it, and a goldsmith overlays it with gold and fashions silver chains for it. [20] A man too poor to present such an offering selects wood that will not rot. He looks for a skilled craftsman to set up an idol that will not topple. [21] Do you not know? Have you not heard? Has it not been told you from the beginning? Have you not understood since the earth was founded? [22] He sits enthroned above the circle of the earth, and its people are like grasshoppers. He stretches out the heavens like a canopy, and spreads them out like a tent to live in. [23] He brings princes to naught and reduces the rulers of this world to nothing. [24] No sooner are they planted, no sooner are they sown, no sooner do they take root in the ground, than he blows on them and they wither, and a whirlwind sweeps them away like chaff. [25] "To whom will you compare me? Or who is my equal?" says the Holy One. [26] Lift your eyes and look to the heavens: Who created all these? He who brings out the starry host one by one, and calls them each by name. Because of his great power and mighty strength, not one of them is missing. [27] Why do you say, O Jacob, and complain, O Israel, "My way is hidden from the LORD; my cause is disregarded by my God"? [28] Do you not know? Have you not heard? The LORD is the everlasting God, the Creator of the ends of the earth. He will not grow tired or weary, and his understanding no one can fathom. [29] He gives strength to the weary and increases the power of the weak. [30] Even youths grow tired and weary, and young men stumble and fall; [31] but those who hope in the LORD will renew their strength. They will soar on wings like eagles; they will run and not grow weary, they will walk and not be faint.

(NIV)

© Belonging to Him Ministries 2009. All rights reserved.

Sitting in Isaiah

Chapter Three   **Lesson One**

Read Isaiah 40. **Key Verse** Isaiah 40:31 "But those who hope in the LORD will renew their strength. They will soar on wings like eagles; they will run and not grow weary, they will walk and not be faint." **Review** this week's key verse and write it on an index card to carry with you to review throughout the day. This week's key verse may already be familiar to you as a verse of comfort and encouragement. You may have learned this verse in a different translation where the word *hope* is rendered *wait*. The word *hope* comes from the Hebrew word *qavah* (kaw-vaw') meaning to expect, to look for patiently, to tarry or to *wait*.

All of us hope for something. Perhaps we hope for less critical things, like an *A* on a test, a promotion, a new purse, a car, or maybe a vacation. We may hope for a miracle to be healed from cancer, to see a marriage restored or a wayward teen come back to Christ. You may hope to save your home from foreclosure, to find a life mate, to be healed from depression, to find a job, to have a child, to see relationships restored, to be loved, to find a friend or to know forgiveness. List things you are waiting and hoping for?

Hope can be a risky proposition if we aren't sure we can trust God to come through for us. Some mistrust God because we have a negative image of Him. Perhaps because we had earthly parents who proved to be untrustworthy God has taken on the faces of those who disappointed and wounded us. Sometimes we feel that God has let us down in the past and even acted unfairly toward us, so trusting Him is difficult for us. If you are new to faith in Christ, perhaps it's difficult for you to trust your heavenly father because you never have until now. Are there things in your life you have difficulty trusting God for? If so, what are they and why is it difficult to trust Him?

© Belonging to Him Ministries 2009. All rights reserved.

Sitting in Isaiah

Judah experienced disappointment with God. They felt that He had failed them when He allowed them to fall into Babylonian captivity in 586 B.C. Even though He had clearly warned them through Isaiah more than 100 years earlier, they brought captivity on themselves (Isaiah 39). Just as Isaiah had prophesied, the refugees would return home from Babylon to find their land stripped bare and ruined. The first 39 chapters of Isaiah are God's warning to them to turn back to Him, but Chapter 40 begins God's message of comfort for them. God gave them the prophetic words through Isaiah that they would need to hear in and after their captivity. They were warned that their sin would have natural consequences and that God would not intervene. It played out exactly that way -- they did not turn back and He did not intervene. Isn't it just like us to blame God when things go badly in our lives?

The question begs asking: "Is God unfair?" We have to come to terms with this question because if we doubt His goodness and fairness it strikes at the core of our belief in Him and will damage our relationship with Him and our ability to put our trust in Him. Have you ever felt that God is unfair? What was the situation?

In his book *Disappointment with God* Philip Yancey looks at this question (Is God unfair?), and he says that "God responded to the question not with words but with a visit, an Incarnation. And Jesus offers flesh-and-blood proof of how God feels about unfairness, for he took on the "stuff" of life, the physical reality at its un-fairest. He gave in summary a final answer to all lurking questions about the goodness of God. No one is exempt from tragedy or disappointment—God himself was not exempt. Jesus offered not immunity, no way out of the unfairness, *but rather a way through it to the other side*. Just as Good Friday demolished the instinctive belief that life is suppose to be fair, Easter Sunday followed with its startling clue to the riddle of the universe. Out of the darkness, a bright light shone. While the cross of Christ overcame evil, it did not overcome unfairness". (Yancey, pp. 215-217)

Life here on earth is unfair. Evil men seem for a time to get away with bad behavior and get richer. Good folks seem to suffer and get poorer. Why doesn't God control everything on the earth so that there is no unfairness? What would our world be like with no choice between good and evil?

© Belonging to Him Ministries 2009. All rights reserved.

Sitting in Isaiah

Having an earthly focus rather than a heavenly one causes us to feel that God is not fair. Heaven is our real home, and our life on earth is our pathway to eternity with our Father. We were created to be with Him, and our time here on earth is our opportunity to get connected with him. If God did control everything on earth then we would all be robots or zombies, with no mind of our own to choose to follow him, or not.

Do you like having your own way with God? Do you ever think so highly of yourself that you think your way is best? Do you want all your prayers answered and for God to do everything for you that you ask, including a front parking space at Target? Do want to be in control of your destiny and but still have Him at your beck and call? Do you feel it is inconvenient when you have to wait for His answers, spend time loving, worship and obeying Him?

Reflect on these questions and confess your answers by way of a prayer in the space below. If you need a fresh wind of faith and confidence in Him to trust Him more deeply for your heart's desires, then ask Him now and write a prayer expressing your concerns and requests to Him.

Optional reading assignment for today: Isaiah Chapter 13.

© Belonging to Him Ministries 2009. All rights reserved.

Sitting in Isaiah

Chapter Three   **Lesson Two**

Read Isaiah 40 in your favorite translation. **Review** this week's key verse Isaiah 40:31. **Read** today's focus verses 1-5. Had Israel received punishment for her sins? Do you think God punishes us for our sins? Is there a difference between discipline and punishment?

The Israelites spent 70 long years in Babylonian captivity, due in part to the natural consequences of their sins and partly due to God's judgment on them as discipline for their sin. They were not ignorant of God's anger toward them. They knew God had had enough, yet they persisted in their sins of practicing idolatry and despising God. We are blessed to live in the new kingdom where Jesus paid the price for our sins, so that we who belong to Christ will never experience the punishment of eternal death for our sins. But there are always natural consequences to our sin because we reap what we sow (Galatians 6:8).

Some of us confuse the unfairness of life on earth with feeling *punished* for our sinful acts. It's not uncommon for some to feel that God is unfair toward them by allowing them to undergo discipline. Like the Israelites, some of us are disappointed in God because we are under His discipline, and His correction has hurt our feelings. Some of us feel unloved by God because of His discipline as a young girl sometimes does under the discipline of her parent. Have you ever felt you were receiving discipline from the Lord? Explain below.

Discipline means tutorage, education, training, or disciplinary correction. The author of the book of Hebrews wisely advises us to take God's correction sincerely and offers us sound advice on how we should view God's discipline. Hebrews 12:5-11 gives seven instructions for our benefit:
1) Do not *scorn* or take it lightly when we are under His discipline
2) Know that His discipline is because He loves us and we are his child
3) Regard His discipline as proof of his love for us
4) Know that His discipline is always for our good

© Belonging to Him Ministries 2009. All rights reserved.

Sitting in Isaiah

5) Regard God's discipline as our training in righteousness, to help us in our struggle against sin and to equip us to resist sin. His discipline may be unpleasant at the time
6) God's discipline will bring a harvest (bounty) of righteousness and peace after we have endured it
7) If we allow ourselves to be bitter toward the Lord we will miss the Grace of God and cause many to be defiled!

How do you know if you are under discipline from the Lord? Have you been a prisoner of sin for which you cannot break free? Are you struggling to resist sin and failing in the struggle? Have you been under a spirit of conviction and repentance? What have you learned about the Lord and yourself through the difficult season?

Write a prayer below, thanking God for his love and attention toward you. Thank Him for Isaiah 40:28 which says "He is the everlasting God who never grows tired or weary *of you*! His understanding *toward you* is unfathomable!" Ask Him to continue to train you so that you don't miss His purpose for you and so you will become all He created you to be!

Optional reading assignment for today: Isaiah Chapter 14.

© Belonging to Him Ministries 2009. All rights reserved.

Sitting in Isaiah

Chapter Three **Lesson Three**

Read all of Isaiah 40 and **review** this week's key verse Isaiah 40:31 by saying it out loud. Today go back one chapter to read Isaiah 39 (it's very short). What were Isaiah's words of warning to King Hezekiah in verse 5-7? What were King Hezekiah's last words recorded in verse 8?

Isaiah 40 reads almost like "back to the future" as Isaiah offers words of encouragement and admonition to Israel for a time yet to come, after their Babylonian captivity of seventy years when they would return to their home land. God summoned the prophet Isaiah "to take a message of hope to his demoralized people" (Ortlund, p. 235). "Little is known about Israel and Judah's life during the captivity. Captivity meant a shameful and humiliating punishment for this disobedient, idolatrous people. The royal court of Judah was taken into captivity, along with the priests, skilled workers, and anyone else who might ever lead a revolt against Babylon. The captives realized that God had finally brought the long-standing covenant curses (Deuteronomy 28:15-68) to bear upon them. Torn from their homes and familiar surroundings, they were forced to travel *900 miles* across a hot desert to a strange land to work as slaves for their conquerors. The punishment of captivity lasted 70 years for Judah; then the penitent were allowed to return to Palestine under the leadership of Ezra and Nehemiah. Israel's tribes, however, never returned and became lost to history. (Lockyer et al.)

We can only imagine how bitterly disappointed the children of Israel must have been not only in themselves for their sinful behavior, but also in their leaders, their ancestors and especially King Hezekiah! He had been warned of their doom and all he seemed to care about was that their destruction wouldn't happen on his watch. Since Hezekiah knew God to be a God of compassion and healing power who healed him in Isaiah 38, could he not have sought the Lord for compassion and healing on his people? Describe a time when you were disappointed in one of your leaders. What brought on your disappointment and what did you learn from it?

© Belonging to Him Ministries 2009. All rights reserved.

Sitting in Isaiah

Living with disappointment in ourselves or others can bring drought, devastation and ruination to our souls. It's hard enough to live with our own sin and mistakes, but a whole different matter when we are forced to bear the painful consequences of another's sin, whether they are a believer, or not. Whether you've been devastated by your own mistakes or someone else's as Beth Moore says "sins are forgiven, but stupid is forever". Receiving forgiveness is the easier part of owning our mistakes or someone else's. The harder work of rebuilding and regaining trust takes time, hard work and consistency.

Recall a time when you were personally affected by the sins of another. How did you make it through that time? How did you survive? Were you able to rebuild trust?

We should be thankful to God because, as Ray Ortlund explains, "if the focus of Christianity were our sins, our future would shut down. But in fact Christianity is all about the saving grace of God. He overrules our stupidity with his own absolute pardon through the finished work of Christ on the cross." (Ortlund, p.235)

When our eyes get off of God we will always experience disillusionment in Him, ourselves or others. Placing our focus on our circumstances, on self or someone else will always lead to disappointment. If we allow ourselves to stay in a pit of discouragement, then disillusionment and discontent will set in, fester and grow. Disappointment easily turns to bitterness. Bitterness unchecked will fester and grow like a cancer, bringing a spiritual drought of overwhelming proportions that our souls can't withstand.

The living water we need for relief from our spiritual drought isn't outside of ourselves. We don't need to change our venue, relationships or church to survive our disappointment. What we need in order to live is found in Isaiah 40:9, "Behold your God…comes! God is always

Sitting in Isaiah

in our desert or our wilderness but sometimes we don't recognize Him. He always comes. In verse 4 He promises to *make a path for you in your wilderness, a highway through your desert, the crooked places will be made straight and the rough ground you stand on made level* (my interpretation). He is God and nothing is too hard for Him. He is everything you need and He will never disappoint.

If you are struggling with disappointment either in yourself or someone else write a prayer asking God to help you refocus your attention on Him. Ask Him to give you grace to forgive. (We will further explore how to forgive later in this study.)

There is extra room for you to journal your struggle and prayers. I exhort you to get it all out before God, Dear One, because He can take whatever complaint or concern you have to share with Him.

Sitting in Isaiah

Spend some quiet reflection in praise and worship for what a great God He is. If you need help refer to Psalm 18, reading it as your prayer of thanksgiving and praise.

Optional reading assignment for today: Isaiah Chapter 15.

Sitting in Isaiah

Chapter Three **Lesson Four**

Read all of Isaiah 40 out loud. **Review** this week's key verse Isaiah 40:31 without looking, from memory. **Re-read** today's focus verses Isaiah 40:9-26 and take note of the characteristics of God listed in this passage. What are we supposed to shout according to verse 9-11 and how does God come into our lives?

Exodus 33:14-18: The LORD replied, "My Presence will go with you, and I will give you rest." Then Moses said to him, "If your Presence does not go with us, do not send us up from here. How will anyone know that you are pleased with me and with your people unless you go with us? What else will distinguish me and your people from all the other people on the face of the earth?" And the LORD said to Moses, "I will do the very thing you have asked, because I am pleased with you and I know you by name." Then Moses said, "Now show me your glory."

What strikes me about this conversation between God and Moses is that Moses could have asked God for anything! God was so pleased with him and offered to do what Moses asked. Can you imagine gaining that kind of opportunity with God? Moses had God's full attention. Exodus 32 reveals how difficult and frustrating it was for Moses to lead the Israelites. He could have asked God to turn them all into sheep, to beam him up to heaven or perhaps just about anything his heart desired. Moses knew full well God's power and understood all too well what God could do! But what Moses asked for astounds me because all he wanted were two things: to be in God's presence and to see His glory.

Max Lucado writes that "When our deepest desire is not the things of God, or a favor from God, but God himself, we cross a threshold. Less self-focus, more God-focus. Less about me, more about him." (Lucado, p. 18). When we face disappointment finding a God-focus is the key to staying on God's pathway of spiritual health and wholeness. Isaiah 40 offers us several key truths to guide us.

© Belonging to Him Ministries 2009. All rights reserved.

Sitting in Isaiah

He is the God who shows up. In Isaiah 40:9 He declares that He is present in our situation and plans to reveal Himself in our wilderness. The display of His glory will be unavoidable to everyone and everything in the world. When God shows up His presence and glory bring joy which refocuses, energizes and excites us, enabling us to get up, get behind Him and follow His lead.

In Isaiah 40:11, what does God promise to do for some of us who are particularly fragile and may have difficulty following Him in our own strength? What does this verse show you about how God views you and your relationship to Him?

He is the all-powerful wise Creator. Write a description below of God's greatness from Isaiah 40:12-17 and 21-26. Explain how this knowledge gives you comfort in your current situation?

God is the only God and an all-knowing God. This truth stands strongly against secularism, the idolatry that dominates our society. It promotes and values skepticism about God from "a general outlook that makes man the measure of all things . . . and reduces God to an object of sentimental indulgence, if he has any place at all." (Ortlund, p. 241) Observe and record how Isaiah 40:13, 14, & 18 exposes the weaknesses of secularism, and reveal that God is the only God and an all knowing God. How does understanding God's omniscience (His all-knowing power) give you comfort today in the midst of our secular culture?

© Belonging to Him Ministries 2009. All rights reserved.

Sitting in Isaiah

Sitting in Isaiah

God is sovereign and in control. This truth stands strongly against the independent, lawless attitude prevalent in our culture that rejects authority of any kind. God's sovereignty means that He has complete, supreme authority and power. How is this core truth revealed in Isaiah 40:10, 21-26. How does knowing this truth change your focus and your view of your current circumstances and your ability to change them?

God has a purpose, plan and agenda for the world. He has graciously allowed you and me to be a part of it. His work is so much bigger than even the most powerful King will ever know. Yet each day He invites you and me to join Him in His work. He is an involved God, aware of everything happening in our life. It's important for us to release God from our ideas of who we think He is and allow Him to manifest Himself to us as He really is.

Write a prayer today asking Him to make these truths real to you so you can experience who He is for yourself.

Optional reading assignment for today: Isaiah Chapter 16.

Sitting in Isaiah

Chapter Three   **Lesson Five**

Read all of Isaiah 40 as a prayer thanking God for His characteristics as listed. **Review** this week's key verse Isaiah 40:31 by writing it from memory. **Re-read** today's focus verses 27-31 and recall a time when you felt that your life was hidden from the Lord (verse 27). The Israelites felt that God had abandoned them by allowing them to fall into captivity. In *The Message* verse 27 reads, "God has lost track of me, he doesn't care what happens to me." If you've ever felt that God lost track of you or doesn't care about you, what happened to cause you to feel that way?

When I was 9 years old my father suddenly and without warning, left our family. He was a local pastor with a thriving church ministry and his unexpected departure left a wake of destruction that devastated a young wife, three young children, our extended family, our immediate and extended church family and our community. The church required us to leave our home, known as the parsonage, soon after to make room for the interim pastor and his family. The intense loss and pain of those first months and years took its toll on me and my family. Words can't even begin to express the feelings of loss and despair. But worse than that was the belief that somehow along the way *God had lost track of me*. I began to believe that what I had learned in Sunday school and from my father's sermons all my life was a lie. I equated the loss of my dad, our home and the misery of our life to mean that God didn't really care about me. A feeling of God-abandonment grew on me like a growth on my shoulder and became extra baggage I carried into adulthood.

This feeling of God-abandonment is what Dr. Sandra Wilson calls "the pain of the pain of abandonment" (Wilson, p. 162). It is bad enough to be wounded and abandoned, but even worse to think that God abandoned us and allowed our wounding. Many of us equate God's

Sitting in Isaiah

love and concern for us with our life experiences. When bad things happen to us we find ourselves often doubting God's love and concern. We wonder if He is too busy, too tired or weary. Have we worn out our welcome mat with God? If God is indeed so big and His plans so grand and we are indeed like grass (verse 6), then what does He want with us? Does He really see and care about what is happening to me?

Have you ever wondered any of these thoughts? If so, what brought them on? What answers do you find in Isaiah 40 that encourage you about how much God cares for you and is in control?

Verse 26 is the key to seeing how important we are to God. *"He brings out the stars one by one, and calls them each by name. Because of his great power and mighty strength, not one of them is missing."* Have you any idea how many stars there are in the heavens? They are not scattered randomly through space but rather they are in vast groupings called galaxies. The Milky Way

Sitting in Isaiah

has our Sun in its galaxy and Astronomers estimate there are about 100 thousand stars just in the Milky Way alone! Beyond the Milky Way there are millions upon millions of other galaxies. If God knows the names and places of millions and millions of stars, then certainly He is able to care about you, to keep you from stumbling and renew your strength! He wants to gather you in His arms and carry you close to His heart!

God's love, compassion, purpose and plan for you are vast. He is an intensely personal God who wants to walk closely with you, reveal Himself to you and show you His glory. But free choice is also His gift to you, He has given you the opportunity to choose to hope and trust in Him, or not.

He knows that you are tired and weary as you make your way through the wilderness of life. Prepare the way for Him, for He comes to make the rough ground level and the crooked places straight!

Write a prayer of thanksgiving and praise from Isaiah 40 and the truths you discovered about Him this week.

Optional reading assignment for today: Isaiah Chapter 17 and 18.

© Belonging to Him Ministries 2009. All rights reserved.

Chapter Four

Isaiah 43

Sitting in Isaiah

Isaiah 43

But now, this is what the LORD says--he who created you, O Jacob, he who formed you, O Israel: "Fear not, for I have redeemed you; I have summoned you by name; you are mine. 2 When you pass through the waters, I will be with you; and when you pass through the rivers, they will not sweep over you. When you walk through the fire, you will not be burned; the flames will not set you ablaze. 3 For I am the LORD, your God, the Holy One of Israel, your Savior; I give Egypt for your ransom, Cush and Seba in your stead. 4 Since you are precious and honored in my sight, and because I love you, I will give men in exchange for you, and people in exchange for your life. 5 Do not be afraid, for I am with you; I will bring your children from the east and gather you from the west. 6 I will say to the north, 'Give them up!' and to the south, 'Do not hold them back. 'Bring my sons from afar and my daughters from the ends of the earth-- 7 everyone who is called by my name, whom I created for my glory, whom I formed and made." 8 Lead out those who have eyes but are blind, who have ears but are deaf. 9 All the nations gather together and the peoples assemble. Which of them foretold this and proclaimed to us the former things? Let them bring in their witnesses to prove they were right, so that others may hear and say, "It is true." 10 "You are my witnesses," declares the LORD," and my servant whom I have chosen, so that you may know and believe me and understand that I am he. Before me no god was formed, nor will there be one after me. 11 I, even I, am the LORD, and apart from me there is no savior. 12 I have revealed and saved and proclaimed--I, and not some foreign god among you. You are my witnesses," declares the LORD, "that I am God. 13 Yes, and from ancient days I am he. No one can deliver out of my hand. When I act, who can reverse it?" 14 This is what the LORD says--your Redeemer, the Holy One of Israel: "For your sake I will send to Babylon and bring down as fugitives all the Babylonians, in the ships in which they took pride. 15 I am the LORD, your Holy One, Israel's Creator, your King." 16 This is what the LORD says--he who made a way through the sea, a path through the mighty waters, 17 who drew out the chariots and horses, the army and reinforcements together, and they lay there, never to rise again, extinguished, snuffed out like a wick: 18 "Forget the former things; do not dwell on the past. 19 See, I am doing a new thing! Now it springs up; do you not perceive it? I am making a way in the desert and streams in the wasteland. 20 The wild animals honor me, the jackals and the owls, because I provide water in the desert and streams in the wasteland, to give drink to my people, my chosen, 21 the people I formed for myself that they may proclaim my praise. 22 "Yet you have not called upon me, O Jacob, you have not wearied yourselves for me, O Israel. 23 You have not brought me sheep for burnt offerings, nor honored me with your sacrifices. I have not burdened you with grain offerings nor wearied you with demands for incense. 24 You have not bought any fragrant calamus for me, or lavished on me the fat of your sacrifices. But you have burdened me with your sins and wearied me with your offenses. 25 "I, even I, am he who blots out your transgressions, for my own sake, and remembers your sins no more. 26 Review the past for me, let us argue the matter together; state the case for your innocence. 27 Your first father sinned; your spokesmen rebelled against me. 28 So I will disgrace the dignitaries of your temple, and I will consign Jacob to destruction and Israel to scorn. (NIV)

© Belonging to Him Ministries 2009. All rights reserved.

Sitting in Isaiah

Chapter Four   **Lesson One**

Read Isaiah 43. **Key Verse** Isaiah 43:18-19, "Forget the former things; do not dwell on the past. See, I am doing a new thing! Now it springs up; do you not perceive it? I am making a way in the desert and streams in the wasteland". **Review** this week's key verse and write it on an index card to carry with you to review throughout the day. Reflect on what this verse means to you and record your thoughts below. To what area of your life do you need to apply this verse?

It is common for us to go through periods of spiritual dryness, like crossing a spiritual desert where nutrients are sparse. The Israelites had grown discouraged as they experienced a spiritual desert with God. He had grown silent toward them. Prior to this time He related to them by revealing Himself frequently in sometimes dramatic ways to prove His existence, love, power and His glory. With His silence and the passage of time they grew cold toward God, as doubt and uncertainty took hold causing them to reach the conclusion that He had abandoned them as we saw in Isaiah 40:27. They filled this void in their lives with other gods (idols) which ultimately led to their destruction.

Do you ever feel discouraged because God seems far from you? Have you ever experienced a spiritual desert? Do you ever have difficulty hearing or seeing Him with your spiritual eyes and ears? Explain below.

Seasons of spiritual dryness can come into our lives for many reasons. We talked about the first one, sin. **Unconfessed sin or a stronghold of sin** deprives the soul of key nutrients for our spiritual health and wholeness. Sin separates us from fellowship with God and blocks our prayers from being heard. Sin is the number one precursor that threatens our spiritual vitality. **Misplaced priorities** are the second factor disaffecting our souls. If we don't make time with

© Belonging to Him Ministries 2009. All rights reserved.

Sitting in Isaiah

God a priority in our life by putting Him before everything else but instead rush our time with Him or perhaps not spend any time with Him we open our souls to a wilderness journey. **Disappointment with God** is a third prominent factor in bringing on a spiritual drought as we discussed last week. **Getting in a rut with God** is another reason that can lead us to a desert. Our key verse speaks to this issue as we often box God into His past patterns of relating to us and aren't open to allowing Him to do new things in our life. When God doesn't reveal Himself to us within the confines of our past experiences of relating with Him we either miss Him altogether or aren't open to the new things He is trying to do in us. The last four factors challenging our spiritual life that will be discussed in the coming weeks are **weariness, loss, isolationism** and our **physical health**. These are key elements in our spiritual health and we will discover how to protect ourselves from spiritual drought when these factors are negatively impacting us.

From the list of causes of spiritual dryness which one is the biggest issue for you and why?

While it may be common to go through a season of spiritual dryness, the condition can take its toll on us, just as it did to the Israelites. When we encounter a spiritual wilderness we must take extra care to protect our selves from the harsh elements and predators that may stalk us during this time of vulnerability. I don't suggest fighting the wilderness experience because I believe our time there can be powerful for our spiritual growth, but I do suggest that when we are in the desert we pay close attention to key principles for our soul's health and safety.

- Believe God regarding Who He says He is and what He says He will do—stand on His character and His promises. If you lack faith, ask Him to give you the spiritual gift of faith to believe Him.

- Never judge God or your condition on the basis of how you feel. Emotions may be true to us but they are not truth we should live by. We should be real with God and others about how we feel, but take great care to not act out of our emotions. Walk in obedience to Him in the truth of His word and make your decisions accordingly.

- Make your time with God a consistent daily priority, both in His Word and in prayer. Meditate and memorize key scriptures that apply to your current life circumstances. Record your struggle in a spiritual journal to document the journey so you can also record His answers.

© Belonging to Him Ministries 2009. All rights reserved.

Sitting in Isaiah

- Fight the urge to be isolated and get into fellowship with believers who will support you in prayer and encourage you in your walk.

- Apply our key verse Isaiah 43:18-19 literally allowing God to answer your prayers and reveal Himself to you in new and unexpected ways. It is common for us to suggest to God *how to answer our concerns*. This limits our ability to see God working, potentially missing His will and the opportunity to experience His glory. We might miss the answer altogether, or become disappointed because we didn't get the answer we were hoping for. All the while, God is still at work and invites us to join Him by bringing just our requests so that we can watch Him work out the answers.

Take advantage of the extra space provided today to reflect on what you have learned. Record your thoughts and insights below asking God to reveal to you how to apply these to your walk with Him. Close your time with Him today redirecting your focus on who He is and what He is done, writing a prayer of thanksgiving and prayer.

Optional reading assignment for today: Isaiah Chapter 19.

Sitting in Isaiah

Chapter Four   **Lesson Two**

Read Isaiah 43. **Review** this week's key verse Isaiah 43:18-19. **Read** today's focus verses 43:1-3. What does God say that He has and will do for you in these three verses? In verse 2 God uses the word *when* which means *with certainty*. From verse 2 what can you be certain you will go through?

Many years ago our family vacationed on the shores of the beautiful Outer Banks of North Carolina. We enjoyed a wonderful time swimming, playing and boogie-boarding in the heavy surf as a hurricane loomed not far away. Not wanting to miss even one day of our vacation, we stayed as long as we could. We knew the beautiful area we were visiting could potentially come under severe flooding and likely be decimated, and it was. The storm surge and rain brought in 20 feet of water and the houses, roads and towns of the Outer Banks community were devastated.

Sometimes loss is like a storm that looms off the coast of our life at a distance. Loss is a part of life and cannot be avoided. Sometimes we know it is near as we wait for the loss to hit us. We prepare as much as possible and we even try to get out of its way. Some times we are fortunate and the looming loss is actually a near-miss and we avoid the destruction. Loss, no matter how big or small accumulates in our soul over time, and if not dwelt with properly will eventually take us down. Whether we loose our job, house, loved one, health, security, fidelity, marriage, friendship, youth, our wedding ring, wallet or our beauty, all loss is painful. What losses have you faced (no matter how big or small) to which you have had difficulty adjusting?

© Belonging to Him Ministries 2009. All rights reserved.

Sitting in Isaiah

What are the promises in Isaiah 43:2 that can encourage and comfort you in a season of loss?

When we loose something we value we experience grief as we face the emptiness and the difficult adjustment to our loss. Grief is the process by which we separate ourselves from the past or from what we lost and begin to replace it with the present with new relationships or new ways of being. If we refuse to resolve our grief, no matter how great or small it is, our soul suffers, and we become angry, bitter and anxious. If we continue denying our losses we run the risk of depleting our soul by becoming vulnerable to food or substance addictions, depression, over-sleeping or insomnia, compulsive behaviors, hypochondria, or worse.

It is common for us to minimize loss and not give grief the attention it deserves. Losses not addressed pile up over time weighing down our soul with pain and grief. Eventually our hearts can't bear any more loss and then one more minor loss sends us over the edge as we crack and break. As an example, it is very common for women who have had an abortion or miscarriage to not allow themselves the time and the focus to grieve. Perhaps they don't feel safe talking and expressing their grief, or maybe they feel that in order to survive, they must deny their loss. Time marches on and when they suffer another loss they aren't able to cope because down deep inside they've never honored the loss that occurred so long ago.

From which losses have you had difficulty recovering?

© Belonging to Him Ministries 2009. All rights reserved.

Sitting in Isaiah

When we lose something important to us we must be honest with God and others. It is good to set a time aside in safe place to grieve, especially on anniversaries of your loss. Allow yourself to feel your loss and accept that your time and energy spent grieving are necessary to the grieving process. Find healthy ways to express your grief. There are many creative ways to express and acknowledge your loss. A few ways are: crying, talking to someone who understands your loss, writing about how you feel, writing a letter to someone who died or left you, finding a memento or keepsake, journaling your memories or lighting candles. It's important to take care to balance our emotions with the Word of God. While you might feel despair and perhaps even that you can't go on, you know from Isaiah 43:2-3 that *God is **with you** and He is the Lord **your** God...**your** Savior.* If you don't have a good support system around you try joining a grief group at your local church or community center. Being able to talk about your loss with those who understand loss will be a great help to you.

Be aware that everyone experiences stages of grief differently. Shock, denial, anger, bargaining, depression and acceptance are all stages of grief but not necessarily always in that order. Allow yourself the gift of grief and honor your loss, whatever it may be.

Use the space provided to share your grief with God and express to him your struggle by way of a prayer. If you have concern for someone else who is hurting, write a prayer for them. Spend some time refocusing your heart on His greatness before you leave your place of prayer today.

Optional reading assignment for today: Isaiah Chapter 20.

© Belonging to Him Ministries 2009. All rights reserved.

Sitting in Isaiah

Chapter Four   **Lesson Three**

Read all of Isaiah 43 observing the phrases that describe who God is. **Review** this week's key verse Isaiah 43:18-19 by writing it from memory. **Re-read** today's focus verses 10-13 and reflect on who God is, what He has done. What does God want us to know, believe and understand? Why?

An idol is anything other than God that we make absolutely essential to our self-image, for peace, contentment, sense of control, or our acceptability (Ortlund, p. 268). The first commandment God gave to His people is found in Exodus 20:3, "You shall have no other gods before me." God went on to clarify what He meant by "no gods" by explaining that "you shall not make for yourself an idol in the form of anything in heaven above or on the earth beneath or in the waters below. You shall not bow down to them or worship them." The pagans engaged in idol worship, serving and bowing to images they carved from wood, stone or hammered metal. The Israelites were influenced by pagan worship and began to practice it while still professing to believe in and worship Jehovah God. They were so brazen in their idol worship that they even brought idols into God's temple!

In the book *No Other Gods,* Kelly Minter writes from 2 Kings 17:33, "They worshiped the Lord, but they also served their own gods." She explains that "God and gods were both occupying space in the jewelry boxes of time, heart and service. The people were living split lives, worshiping One while serving the other." She adds, "perhaps so many of our struggles—lack of freedom, loss of spiritual desire, slavery to image, perfectionism, confusion and the list is infinite—had much to do with this idea of God and gods…" She writes further, "Whatever we depend upon we will most certainly serve. If our false gods have taken up our most treasured spaces, we leave God no place to show Himself strong on our behalf" (pp. 45-46).

In Exodus 20:3 the word *your* is "the one word that changes everything, the word that brings what could have been a faceless God into a reachable One, the word that sparks the question

© Belonging to Him Ministries 2009. All rights reserved.

Sitting in Isaiah

'Is he God, or is he your God?' And if he is God, but not your God, I would like to propose that it's a relationship not strong enough to keep you from false gods. If we're not in personal relationship with Him we will absolutely be in it with something else, a false god, because our hearts were designed in such a way as to be intimate with something." God is a personal God and He won't be satisfied with anything less than a personal relationship with those He created in His image (Sailhamer, p. 285).

Many of us play the part of a Christian well, sometimes even fooling ourselves. We go to church, study the Bible and witness to others, but what really keeps us going is our false gods that we rely heavily upon for strength and security. We naturally gravitate towards whatever we feel will fill us and make us happy. We believe the lie that God really isn't enough, and so we live for both God and gods. Friends, boyfriends, husbands, family, houses, cars, wealth, sex, pleasure, recreation, education, beauty, the body….or whatever it is that will give us the freedom, significance, and security we require to feel okay about ourselves and our life. Recognizing our idol worship is perhaps the easier part, but changing our patterns of thinking and behaving is altogether a different challenge. Idolatry is a stronghold behind which other strongholds follow. Virtually every stronghold involves the worship of some kind of idol. (Beth Moore, *Praying God's Word,* p. 20)

Are you aware of idolatry in your life? Reflect on what your idols are and write a prayer of confession below.

Sitting in Isaiah

Our sin problem is really a symptom of our deeper problem, idolatry. Our patterns of sin stem from our idols because we will serve what we worship. The problem is that we expect so little of God because we aren't connected to Him on a deeply personal level because we haven't made Him *our God*. To be able to know and see God as our own God we must have some kind of experience with Him. Whether you came to Christ today or ten years ago, it means you have a history with Him and a story to tell.

Write your story below. What has God done for you? What has he delivered you from? How has he changed you? You may want to answer these questions by way of a prayer.

Sitting in Isaiah

If you have never formally made a commitment to make God YOUR God, I encourage you to do that today and don't wait. Use the space provided to write a prayer of commitment or recommitment to Him. Share your decision with a trusted friend or spiritual leader.

Optional reading assignment for today: Isaiah Chapter 21.

© Belonging to Him Ministries 2009. All rights reserved.

Sitting in Isaiah

Chapter Four   **Lesson Four**

Read all of Isaiah 43 in your favorite translation. **Review** this week's key verse Isaiah 43:18-19 by saying it out loud. Read today's focus verses 22-24 and notice the use of the words *wearied and burdened*. Reflect on what causes you to feel weary or burdened?

Weariness is one of the key causes of burn-out. When our souls get run down, tired and exhausted, we become vulnerable to spiritual drought and burn-out. Wounds from rejection are a primary contributing factor that wearies the soul over time.

We must live real and authentic lives to be healthy, but because we fear that being real may mean we won't be accepted for who we really are, we easily slip into a pattern of false living. False living is self-protective living in order to earn approval and protection from the wounds of rejection. Whether you experience rejection from someone you deeply love and admire or from someone you hardly know, repeated rejection can mortally wound our soul!

The natural way we try protecting ourselves from rejection is two-fold. The first is by *performing*. We try to be what we perceive others around us want us to be (perfect) so they won't have any reason to criticize, reject or abandon us. We learn to masterfully assess every situation we are in (sometimes we even do this unconsciously) and adjust ourselves to what those around us want from us, in order to be fully accepted by them. Living a performance-perfectionistic life means that we are forever changing our personalities to fit the needs of the group we are in. Some of us have multiple personality styles that we put on at any given moment. We have our social style, our friendship style, our work personality, our church personality, our neighborhood style of relating and then our private home life. Living for approval so that we won't be rejected is not only draining and nearly impossible to keep up, but more importantly, *it is a sin* because it is inauthentic or hypocritical living.

Are you weary from being a people pleaser? Can you think of some ways that you may be living for approval of others so that you won't have to endure rejection from them? Explain below.

© Belonging to Him Ministries 2009. All rights reserved.

Sitting in Isaiah

The second way we try to insulate ourselves from rejection is to *put our real selves in jail*. Some of us are so certain that our real selves will be an instant disappointment to others that we have thrown away the key to our jail cell so that we never face our real selves again! Sometimes our real self has been jailed so long we can't remember what we looked like! The habit of *faking it*, of holding our real self captive from those around us in order to protect ourselves from rejection, is not only completely exhausting and depleting to the health of the soul—*it is also a sin* because it is denying the goodness of what God has made.

I am more than aware of how painful it is when we don't like our real selves but we need to be real so God can change us into the person He created us to be.

Reflect on these truths for a moment. Are there tangible ways you have jailed your real self, holding back so that others might like you better? Explain below and write a prayer of confession asking God for His clarity.

Sitting in Isaiah

The reason rejection is so deeply wounding to our soul is because we were created to find *complete acceptance and love* from our Abba (Daddy) Father. To know approval, acceptance and complete belonging for who we really are, down to the very core of our soul is the deepest most basic need we have. We must know that *God created us with this need so that He could and would meet it!*

It is hard to give up the act and start living in God's approval as the measure for everything we do and say! We might want to take it slow when we begin to let our real selves out of jail! Our true self might not have been allowed to relate for many years, so it might take a little practice in the beginning to learn to be vulnerable in a safe and tactful way. We should be prepared for more rejection in the beginning as we learn to express our real self, aware that we might upset those around us who don't actually know us because we haven't been authentic up until now.

Are there people in your life from whom you seek approval? Are you afraid to be yourself because of the power of rejection and control they hold over you? List their initials below and write a prayer asking God to give you the strength to be real with them in the gentleness of the Holy Spirit and with the love of God.

We are all in process. Being real with God and others helps us to speed the process along because God can begin to really work in us as we give ourselves up to Him. When we come to Christ we are given the gift of the Holy Spirit and spiritual gifts as well. Being free to use our spiritual gifting and express the fruit of the Spirit is the way we allow God to be glorified in us. When we live for the approval of others and lock up our real selves we deny who God is

Sitting in Isaiah

and don't allow Him to shine through us. But when we set our security in Him and Him alone, allowing Him to show us how much He accepts, loves and sees us for *who and how* we truly are, we bring Him magnificent glory!

Spend a few moments in quiet reflection asking God to reveal truth to you in the inmost secret places of your soul. Record your conversation with Him and thank Him for His great unchanging magnificent love for you.

Optional reading assignment for today: Isaiah Chapter 22.

Sitting in Isaiah

Chapter Four   **Lesson Five**

Read all of Isaiah 43 out loud. **Review** this week's key verse Isaiah 43:18-19 without looking, from memory. **Re-read** today's focus verses 23-24 and reflect on verse 23b. From *The Message* God says; "It wasn't that I asked that much from you, I didn't expect expensive presents." In yesterday's lesson we discussed performing and faking it in order to gain acceptance from others. Are there times when you feel you have to work to earn God's love, approval and acceptance? What would Jesus say about this?

Growing up as a PK's (pastor's kid) our life as a family was generally lived in a fish bowl. Everything we did was under the microscope. Appearances were everything. But even perfectionism didn't feel like it was good enough. I grew up with the overwhelming sense that nothing I did, nor how I looked, was ever good enough. In fairness to other ministry families I need to say that it wasn't being a PK that caused the perfectionism syndrome, but the dysfunction in my family. Being a PK only exacerbated the intense feelings of performing and faking it for the sake of approval and acceptance.

Many of us understand the pressure of growing up with this type of dysfunction. The hard part is what we call *transference*. When we grow up faking and performing for our parents and care givers so that we will feel loved and accepted we can easily transfer their images onto God's image. In other words, we can't accept God's love and acceptance as free gifts but feel we must work to earn His approval. So when we accept Christ we continue performing and faking it for Him too.

It is so hard for us to fully comprehend God's love and acceptance of us. He tells us that when we are in Christ we are already a new creation, the old has passed and the new has come. Christ's righteousness is imputed to us so that God is able to look at us completely free from sin. We are clean in His eyes. Isaiah 43:13 he says "no one can deliver out of my hand. When I act, who can reverse it?" And in John 10:29-30 Jesus says, My Father, who has given them to Me, is greater than all; and no one is able to snatch them out of My Father's hand. I and My Father are one." No one and nothing can separate us from God's love for us (Romans 8:38). We are free to be real with God about our insecurities and approval addiction. We honor God with our honesty.

© Belonging to Him Ministries 2009. All rights reserved.

Sitting in Isaiah

Many religions are legalistic and teach performance as a way of gaining salvation and favor with God. But Ephesians 2:8-9 says that we cannot earn our salvation or His favor, it is a gift from God. Many scriptures teach that God loves and accepts us for whom and how we are because of Jesus and His saving work for us at Calvary. But simply memorizing scriptures isn't going to change our behavior. To experience real life-altering change we have to have a head-to-heart connection. Life-altering change only occurs through spending time with our heavenly Father allowing Him to minister His word in the very depths of our soul in our relationship with Him. In her book *Into Abba's Arms*, Dr. Sandra Wilson calls this "experiencing transforming truth *relationally*.... The indispensible condition for developing and maintaining the awareness of our belovedness is time alone with God." (p. 97)

We will likely be weary, drought-stricken, burnt-out, depleted Christians if we spend our energy working for God and serving Him not because we love Him so much but because we want to make sure He approves of us. We will be tempted to burn the candle at both ends because we not only want to feel we've earned God's favor but also the favor of other believer's. Approval addiction is a pit and a trap of the enemy.

If you realize today that you aren't feeling very secure with God, write a prayer telling Him your struggle. End this week's lesson recalling truths from Isaiah 43 that have convinced you of His great love and acceptance of you.

Optional reading assignment for today: Isaiah Chapter 23 and 24.

© Belonging to Him Ministries 2009. All rights reserved.

Chapter Five

Isaiah 25

Sitting in Isaiah

Isaiah 25

O LORD, you are my God; I will exalt you and praise your name, for in perfect faithfulness you have done marvelous things, things planned long ago. ² You have made the city a heap of rubble, the fortified town a ruin, the foreigners' stronghold a city no more; it will never be rebuilt. ³ Therefore strong peoples will honor you; cities of ruthless nations will revere you. ⁴ You have been a refuge for the poor, a refuge for the needy in his distress, a shelter from the storm and a shade from the heat. For the breath of the ruthless is like a storm driving against a wall ⁵ and like the heat of the desert. You silence the uproar of foreigners; as heat is reduced by the shadow of a cloud, so the song of the ruthless is stilled. ⁶ On this mountain the LORD Almighty will prepare a feast of rich food for all peoples, a banquet of aged wine--the best of meats and the finest of wines. ⁷ On this mountain he will destroy the shroud that enfolds all peoples, the sheet that covers all nations; ⁸ he will swallow up death forever. The Sovereign LORD will wipe away the tears from all faces; he will remove the disgrace of his people from all the earth. The LORD has spoken. ⁹ In that day they will say, "Surely this is our God; we trusted in him, and he saved us. This is the LORD, we trusted in him; let us rejoice and be glad in his salvation." ¹⁰ The hand of the LORD will rest on this mountain; but Moab will be trampled under him as straw is trampled down in the manure. ¹¹ They will spread out their hands in it, as a swimmer spreads out his hands to swim. God will bring down their pride despite the cleverness of their hands. ¹² He will bring down your high fortified walls and lay them low; he will bring them down to the ground, to the very dust.

(NIV)

Sitting in Isaiah

Chapter Five   **Lesson One**

Read Isaiah 25. **Key Verse** Isaiah 25:1 "O LORD, you are my God; I will exalt you and praise your name, for in perfect faithfulness you have done marvelous things, things planned long ago". **Review** this week's key verse and write it on an index card to carry with you to review throughout the day. What are some ways that God's faithfulness to His children is revealed in Isaiah 25? Make a list below.

In the last chapter we discussed idolatry and how "it is a stronghold for which all other strongholds follow close behind. Virtually every stronghold involves the worship of some kind of idol" (Moore, *Praying God's Word*, p. 20). Now, in Isaiah 25 we will see what a stronghold is and then take a look at four formidable strongholds that challenge a believer's spiritual growth. You may be surprised given Isaiah's positive and victorious tone in this chapter that it would lead us to discuss the strongholds of unbelief, the enemy, unforgiveness and pride. Isaiah 25 describes the "after" picture, and to appreciate it we need to ask about and see what the "before" picture looks like. What is the actual overcoming work that Isaiah is praising God for?

The word stronghold appears only one time in the New Testament, and it means a fortress, or some other thing in which human confidence is placed. It is found in 2 Corinthians 10:3-5:
> "For though we live in the world, we do not wage war as the world does. The weapons we fight with are not the weapons of the world. On the contrary, they have divine power to demolish *strongholds*. We demolish *arguments and every pretension* that sets itself up against the knowledge of God, and we take captive every thought to make it obedient to Christ." (italics added for emphasis)

A stronghold is anything that exalts itself in our minds, anything that *pretends* (pretension) or asserts itself as being stronger or bigger or more believable than God (this is idolatry). Strongholds form in us when we develop a habitual sin, often in an area of vulnerability, and that sin becomes fortified in us and a part of us. A pattern of ungodly behavior sets in and we struggle to control our actions, reactions, emotions and responses that we know are wrong.

© Belonging to Him Ministries 2009. All rights reserved.

Sitting in Isaiah

Strongholds steal our focus away from God, causing us to feel over-powered on the battlefield of our mind, which brings defeat because what we think about we bring about. A stronghold "is something that consumes so much of our emotional and mental energy that abundant life is strangled—our callings remain largely unfulfilled and our believing lives are virtually ineffective. Needless to say, these are the enemy's precise goals" (Moore, *Praying God's Word*, p. 3). If we don't armor up, Satan just needs to poke us and our wounds open up again.

Are you aware of the strongholds that are working against you? Write a prayer confessing any stronghold that you face. If you aren't sure, ask God to reveal truth to you. Wait on Him for His answer. Ask God to begin a new work in you to tear down and demolish any argument or stronghold that is set up against Him and help you to break free.

The most effective way for the enemy to change our behavior and get us misbehaving is to tempt us to think negative thoughts. Because Satan is a loser, already defeated in the end game, his way of messing with our thought life is by pretending with us. His goal is getting us to break from reality with him and to believe in and act on something that is not true—but a lie. Our goals in understanding what a stronghold is and how to demolish it are to take back our own thought life, re-claim every thought for Christ and line up all of our thinking with the truth of the Word of God. Think of it as downsizing whatever might be overpowering you and bringing it under Christ's authority.

Because strongholds follow so closely behind the sin of idolatry, as Beth Moore exhorts us, we must be aware that:
> "as long as our minds rehearse the strength of our stronghold more than the strength of our God, we will be impotent ... we may be forced to realize that our perception of God is something that we ourselves have conjured up and not the one true God at all ... *we may have carved a 'god' out of our own image or imagination, giving him human or noble characteristics*" (Moore, *Praying God's Word*, pp. 20-21).

© Belonging to Him Ministries 2009. All rights reserved.

Sitting in Isaiah

We have two weapons for demolishing strongholds: the Word of God and prayer.

- Begin by asking God to give you **a willing heart** because honestly, some of us like our strongholds and don't want to give them up! (Psalm 51:12).
- God desires you to know truth in the inmost part of your soul, so you can **ask Him to show you** what your strongholds are (Psalm 139:23-24; Psalm 51:6).
- With the Holy Spirit's help **acknowledge, recognize or identify** your strongholds (John 16:8).
- Spend time in prayer in **confession and repentance** (2 Corinthians 7:10; 1 John 1:9).
- **Renew the mind** with scriptures that apply specifically to your struggle. It's important to choose new thoughts through applying specific scripture. We can't just empty our mind of a wrong thought without having a scripturally correct thought to replace it (James 1:22; Ephesians 4:23). This is one reason why we should memorize Bible verses.
- Lastly but most importantly, don't just speak the Word of God, but **pray the Word of God** (Ephesians 6:18; Isaiah 55:11)! God's Word will never return to Him void (Isaiah 55:11). There is so much healing power in the Word of God that can lead us to victory.

Use the space provided to follow these steps, recording your conversation with God regarding your strongholds. Write your prayer for His help in breaking free.

Ephesians 6:18 - "And pray in the Spirit on all occasions with all kinds of prayers and requests. With this in mind, be alert and always keep on praying for all the saints."

Optional reading assignment for today: Isaiah Chapter 26.

Sitting in Isaiah

Chapter Five **Lesson Two**

Read Isaiah 25 and take note of God's completed action items. **Review** this week's key verse Isaiah 25:1. What action did God take on behalf of His children that encourages you most today?

Unbelief can become a pervasive stronghold that affects our ability to overcome all other strongholds, making it literally impossible to break free if we don't believe God. A stronghold of unbelief is toxic to our soul and will pollute our foundation of faith if not dealt with. Last week you read Isaiah 43 many times and we touched briefly on the word *believe* in verse 10.

In Hebrew (as in Isaiah 43:10) and Greek (as in Luke 1:4) the word *believe* means nearly the same. In the Hebrew it conveys a picture of fostering like a nurse or a parent. I love this definition because it demonstrates that we must continue to protect and pursue our belief in God, undergird it with truth and actively support it with prayer and time spent with Him. For example, even though I know and believe that my mother loves me, it doesn't mean I don't need to nurture that belief by spending time with her and hearing her confirm her love for me! It is the same in our relationship with God.

What does God say He wants us to do in Isaiah 43:10?

God wants us to know Him, believe Him, and understand Him. Not believe *in* Him, **but believe Him**, period. Jesus taught the importance of this point in Mark 9:14-24. A man brought his son to Jesus. The boy had been possessed by a demon for years and no one had been able to help them. The boy and his family had no doubt been tortured, suffering untold loss and pain due to his frightening condition. Jesus was their last hope. The father asked Jesus, "If you can do

© Belonging to Him Ministries 2009. All rights reserved.

Sitting in Isaiah

anything..." Jesus said, "If you can? Everything is possible for him who believes." The father's immediate response is God's encouragement to us now that honest confession brings healing and power into our lives. The father cried out to Jesus, "I do believe; help me overcome my unbelief!" Jesus healed his son, but even more than that, Jesus dealt with the deeper issue, that of unbelief. This story demonstrates that God isn't interested in pious platitudes but rather honest pleas for what we need.

In what areas do you struggle to believe God? Is it His total love and complete acceptance of you? For His power, His mercy, His answer? Reflect in prayer on these questions asking Him to reveal truth about yourself to you. Record your holy conversation below.

Ephesians 1:18-19 tells us that "God wields incomparably great power to those of us who believe and then He applies that same power to our need that he exerted when He raised Christ from the dead." To know and experience this power we must believe God, that "He can do what He says He can do. Believe you can do what He says you can do. Believe He is who He says He is. And believe you are who he says you are" (Moore, *Praying God's Word*, p. 35).

Believing these truths will not keep you out of the storms of life. God will use the storms of life to test your belief and faith in Him and produce great fruit in you. You will be challenged to believe Him for your remaining days on this earth. The difference will be whether you lack faith due to a stronghold of unbelief or because you succumbed to a moment of discouragement?

Sitting in Isaiah

Demolishing the stronghold of unbelief is hard work, just as for any stronghold, so it's important to ask God for a willing heart. Ask Him to show you your unbelief and give you more faith. Acknowledge and confess your unbelief, renewing your mind with Scriptures and praying them back to God. Use the space provided to reflect on today's lesson. These steps to breaking free may need to be repeated until you are released from the stronghold.

Optional reading assignment for today: Isaiah Chapter 27.

Sitting in Isaiah

Chapter Five   **Lesson Three**

Read all of Isaiah 25. **Review** this week's key verse Isaiah 25:1 by writing it from memory. **Re-read** today's focus verse 4 and notice the word *refuge* which means a fortified place, a defense. Don't you just love the picture of God as both a place of defense for the poor, needy and distressed as well as a shelter? The word *distress* comes from the Hebrew word tsar (tsar) which means a tight place or trouble. Have you ever been poor, needy or in distress? Reflect on how God helped you and how God has been your refuge?

A stronghold of the enemy is a ruthless, oppressive force that can completely overcome us and defy our ability to break free in our own strength. It can come when we open a doorway to evil and give the enemy open access into our lives. A stronghold of the enemy can take on many forms including depression, addiction, fear of rejection, despair, idolatry, unbelief. God's Word is clear that we are to stand and fight the good fight of faith against the evil one (Ephesians 6), and so today we will look at how to do just that. Beth Moore exhorts us in her book *Praying God's Word to* "give much time and thought to becoming well-equipped victors in the battle that rages, but give *more* time to the pursuit of the heart of God and all things concerning Him. Much about warfare. *More about God Himself*" (p. 311).

It is vital to understand that God has not given us a spirit of fear, and so it is our position of peace along with the Word and prayer that defeats Satan. If we fear Satan we give him glory. We also glorify Satan when we blame everything that goes wrong on him. He loves it when we talk about him like that. We give Satan access when we don't armor-up and recognize him as our opponent.

Satan is a schemer and he is cunning so there may be times we are under attack and don't realize it! That is precisely why we need each other.

In Matt 4:1-11 we see how Jesus faced Satan and resisted the enemy from establishing a stronghold. With every temptation He rebuked Satan with the Word of God. Satan didn't scram until Jesus told him to get away! Because of Jesus we have the power and authority

© Belonging to Him Ministries 2009. All rights reserved.

Sitting in Isaiah

to rebuke Satan but we must put on the full armor of God first (Ephesians 6). As in Isaiah 25 where God delivers His people from ruthless enemies, God can deliver us from strongholds of the enemy. God has put everything under the authority of Jesus and as we live under His authority "all of the enemy's powers are now under our feet" (Myers, *31 Days of Power*, p. 113).

If you are convinced or even suspicious that you are under a stronghold of the enemy begin by following the steps from lesson one on breaking down a stronghold.
- Ask God to give you a willing heart to face your stronghold (Psalm 51:12)
- Ask God to reveal truth to you by his Holy Spirit (Psalm 51:6; Psalm 139:23-24)
- Confess and repent any known sin (2 Corinthians 7:10)
- Renew your mind with suggested Scriptures listed below
- Pray the Word of God daily against your stronghold until you feel released. It's a good idea to routinely pray what I call "maintenance prayers" against strongholds from which you have broken free.

Scriptures for overcoming a stronghold of evil: Exodus 3:14-15; Exodus 15; Psalm 16:1-2; 17:7-9; 18:1-3, 4-6, 16-19; Luke 22:31; John 10:10; John 14:30; John 17:15; Romans 16:20; 2 Corinthians 6:15, 11:14, 3:14-16, Ephesians 6:10-18; Philippians 4:5-9; 1 Peter 5:8-9; 1 John 4:1-4; Revelation 12:10-12; Revelation 20:10.

In the space provided below, begin your prayer journey in breaking down a stronghold of the enemy. If you are not under a stronghold of the enemy, praise God for His keeping and use the space below to pray for someone you suspect may be suffering with this kind of stronghold.

Optional reading assignment for today: Isaiah Chapter 28.

© Belonging to Him Ministries 2009. All rights reserved.

Sitting in Isaiah

Chapter Five **Lesson Four**

Read all of Isaiah 25 in your favorite translation. **Review** this week's key verse Isaiah 25:1 by saying it out loud. Read today's focus verse Hebrews 12:15 "See to it that no one misses the grace of God and that no bitter root grows up to cause trouble and defile many."

All strongholds must be demolished, broken down, in order for us to be free. But the stronghold of unforgiveness is perhaps one of the hardest. When we withhold forgiveness, a root of bitterness grows in us and begins to affect every area of our life. If allowed to continue it toxifies the soul. Left to fester, the soul is starved of key life giving nutrients. Bitterness of the soul makes us spiritually, emotionally and even physically ill. We can all relate to facing overwhelming circumstances that are difficult, perhaps seeming almost impossible to forgive. And then there are certain offenses that seem to be unforgiveable. Some of us still have relationships with those who have rejected, abandoned or betrayed us, and who continue to hurt us. Others live with the pain left behind by someone who died before forgiveness could be realized. How do you reconcile with a corpse? Living with this type of wounding makes it very hard to forgive.

Is there someone you have struggled to forgive? Reflect on why it has been so hard for you to be free from the wounding and have complete forgiveness? If you aren't sure of the answer, ask God to show you.

God commands us to forgive (Colossians 3:13). God does not qualify the command by saying to only forgive those who seek forgiveness, or who confess and admit their sins, or who have repented and turned away from their sins. God tells us we must forgive, period. One reason we withhold forgiveness is that we don't understand it. In her book *Into Abba's Arms*, Dr. Sandra Wilson defines forgiveness by what it is *not*.

- **Forgiveness does not excuse the offender** and is not saying that what you did to me is no big deal. It is a big deal because it hurt you!

© Belonging to Him Ministries 2009. All rights reserved.

Sitting in Isaiah

- When we forgive **it doesn't mean that we will now live as if the painful experience never happened**. It did happen and we can't erase it, nor should we try.
- **Forgiving is not the cliché** *forgive and forget.* (Who made that up anyway? It's not in the Bible!) It takes time to heal our wounds and our memory, and there are some things that we will never forget. Forgiving doesn't mean we suddenly develop a case of amnesia.
- **Forgiveness is not the same as trusting.** Trust is rebuilt over time and it is important and healthy to set boundaries and proceed with caution when working to restore a broken relationship. How often have you heard someone say "if you don't trust me then you haven't forgiven me?!" Often we must forgive those who refuse to take any responsibility for their actions.
- Our **forgiveness is not based on their repentance. Forgiving those who betrayed us isn't something we can do alone.** "Deeply transforming experiences of forgiveness are humanly impossible—without the Spirit of God." (Wilson, p.167)
- **Unless God empowers our decision to forgive we won't stay with the hard work that forgiveness requires.**
- **Forgiveness is giving up the right to wrong those who have wronged us.** It is also refusing to be 'overcome by evil' (Roman 12:21) by getting stuck in bitterness and resentment. (Wilson, pp. 163-169).

Reflect on Dr. Wilson's definition of forgiveness and record your insights on truth you learned and how you might need to apply that to your life. What is the most difficult part of forgiveness for you? Record your prayer below.

Optional reading assignment for today: Isaiah Chapter 29.

© Belonging to Him Ministries 2009. All rights reserved.

Sitting in Isaiah

Chapter Five   **Lesson Five**

Read all of Isaiah 25 out loud as a prayer. **Review** this week's key verse Isaiah 25:1 without looking, from memory. **Re-read** today's focus verses 10-12 and insert the word "pride" for Moab and "you or your" for "they or them". Reflect on what God will do with pride and the prideful fortified walls.

The stronghold of pride is the last stronghold that we will discuss as a factor in what brings drought, ruin and devastation to the soul. Pride is toxic to the soul because it is an empty lie. Pride is a false sense of confidence that blocks our connection to the only solution to our deepest needs. "Pride brings immense loss to God because it deprives Him of the genuine intimacy with us that he longs for" (Myers, *31 Days of Prayer*, p. 192).

Beth Moore says, "The most effective means the enemy has to keep believers from being full of the spirit is to keep us full of ourselves." "God won't put up with pride in His own children very long without dealing with it." "Pride is the opposite of humility … *but it* is not the opposite of low self-esteem." People with serious low self-esteem issues definitely have a serious pride problem. "Pride is self-absorption whether we are absorbed with how miserable we are or how wonderful we are." "If we don't presently have an issue that is actively humbling us, we veer with disturbing velocity toward arrogance and self-righteousness." (Moore, *Praying God's Word*, p.57-58)

Write your own definition of what you think it means to have a stronghold of pride.

Understanding pride, what it is and how to recognize it is a little easier than understanding what humility is. If we can understand and recognize humility we will more easily see pride when it rears its ugly head. Humility has nothing to do with being weak or pessimistic. It is simply thinking about God and ourselves realistically. Our failures and unmet needs are in reality great blessings in disguise. ***They remind us that we are not qualified to run our own lives.*** They press us to commit ourselves to Christ and trust Him (Myers, *31 Days of Prayer*, p. 192).

© Belonging to Him Ministries 2009. All rights reserved.

Sitting in Isaiah

Humility is freedom from arrogance that grows out of the recognition that all we have and are comes from God. It is typically confused with the belittling of oneself. This is called false humility. True humility is recognition that by ourselves we are inadequate, without dignity and worthless. Yet, because we are created in God's image and because believers are in Christ, we have infinite worth and dignity (1 Corinthians 4:6-7; 1 Peter 1:18-19). True humility does not produce pride but gratitude. Since God is both our Creator and Redeemer, our existence and righteousness depend upon Him (John 15:5; Acts 17:28; Ephesians 2:8-10). (Lockyer et al.)

Write your own definition of humility below.

If we want God to work in us, speak to us and answer our prayers, then humility is not merely a nice extra, it is essential. "God opposes the proud, but gives grace to the humble…blessed are the destitute and helpless in the realm of the spirit for theirs is the kingdom of heaven (James 4:6; Matthew 5:3)

Spend a few moments in listening prayer, asking God to reveal to you any strongholds that you may be harboring. Record your holy conversation in the space provided. I encourage you to end your prayer time with praise and thanksgiving to refocus your thoughts and emotions "lest Satan should take advantage of (you) us; for (you) we are not ignorant of his devices (2 Corinthians 2:11, NKJV).

Optional reading assignment for today: *Isaiah Chapter* 30-31.

© Belonging to Him Ministries 2009. All rights reserved.

Chapter Six

Isaiah 58

Sitting in Isaiah

Isaiah 58

"Shout it aloud, do not hold back. Raise your voice like a trumpet. Declare to my people their rebellion and to the house of Jacob their sins. ² For day after day they seek me out; they seem eager to know my ways, as if they were a nation that does what is right and has not forsaken the commands of its God. They ask me for just decisions and seem eager for God to come near them. ³ 'Why have we fasted,' they say, 'and you have not seen it? Why have we humbled ourselves, and you have not noticed?' "Yet on the day of your fasting, you do as you please and exploit all your workers. ⁴ Your fasting ends in quarreling and strife, and in striking each other with wicked fists. You cannot fast as you do today and expect your voice to be heard on high. ⁵ Is this the kind of fast I have chosen, only a day for a man to humble himself? Is it only for bowing one's head like a reed and for lying on sackcloth and ashes? Is that what you call a fast, a day acceptable to the LORD? ⁶ "Is not this the kind of fasting I have chosen: to loose the chains of injustice and untie the cords of the yoke, to set the oppressed free and break every yoke? ⁷ Is it not to share your food with the hungry and to provide the poor wanderer with shelter--when you see the naked, to clothe him, and not to turn away from your own flesh and blood? ⁸ Then your light will break forth like the dawn, and your healing will quickly appear; then your righteousness will go before you, and the glory of the LORD will be your rear guard. ⁹ Then you will call, and the LORD will answer; you will cry for help, and he will say: Here am I. "If you do away with the yoke of oppression, with the pointing finger and malicious talk, ¹⁰ and if you spend yourselves in behalf of the hungry and satisfy the needs of the oppressed, then your light will rise in the darkness, and your night will become like the noonday. ¹¹ The LORD will guide you always; he will satisfy your needs in a sun-scorched land and will strengthen your frame. You will be like a well-watered garden, like a spring whose waters never fail. ¹² Your people will rebuild the ancient ruins and will raise up the age-old foundations; you will be called Repairer of Broken Walls, Restorer of Streets with Dwellings. ¹³ "If you keep your feet from breaking the Sabbath and from doing as you please on my holy day, if you call the Sabbath a delight and the LORD's holy day honorable, and if you honor it by not going your own way and not doing as you please or speaking idle words, ¹⁴ then you will find your joy in the LORD, and I will cause you to ride on the heights of the land and to feast on the inheritance of your father Jacob." The mouth of the LORD has spoken.

(NIV)

Sitting in Isaiah

Chapter Six   **Lesson One**

Read Isaiah 58. **Key Verse** Isaiah 58:8-9a "Then your light will break forth like the dawn, and your healing will quickly appear; then your righteousness will go before you, and the glory of the LORD will be your rear guard. Then you will call, and the LORD will answer; you will cry for help, and he will say: Here am I." **Review** this week's key verse and write it on an index card to carry with you to review throughout the day.

Make note of God's promises in the key verses. Keeping in the context with Isaiah 58, are these promises conditional? Do they depend on us in order for them to be fulfilled for us?

It is true that God's love and many of His promises are unconditional, but in this passage He is very clear that our healing and wholeness depends in a large part upon us. Living a life in Christ that is rejuvenated and in good spiritual health is dependent upon us just as much as it is on God. The message of Isaiah 58 is clear, we need to clean up our hearts and our lives in order to live restored and refreshed.

Everyone wants to experience the promises of verses 8-9. Everywhere you turn today you cannot escape information about good health, ultimate wholeness and natural ways of healing the body, mind and spirit. The problem and danger is that we look for wholeness in all the wrong places. Our spiritual health and wholeness isn't found in the world, but in God alone. Restoration, renovation, sanctification and rejuvenation all lie in one source, our Father God through His son Jesus. To experience these we must experience revival.

What advice do you commonly hear from the world on how to be rejuvenated and refreshed?

The word revive is used only twice in one verse of the book of Isaiah. Isaiah 57:17 says, "I live in a high and holy place, but also with him who is contrite and lowly in spirit, to

© Belonging to Him Ministries 2009. All rights reserved.

Sitting in Isaiah

revive the spirit of the lowly and to *revive* the heart of the contrite". *Revive* means to give life, make alive, to quicken."

My parents participated in many revival crusades which my young brothers and I were required to attend. We would often stay late into the night watching the adults praying, crying and waiting on God. As a child all I seemed to come away with were sore feet from too small of shoes, a sore behind from sitting so long, great hunger pains and overly tired of the whole experience. And it looked to me like I wasn't the only one in misery!

We can't force revival upon ourselves or others! It can't be artificially induced. We can and should pray, expect and look for revival as long as we understand that revival comes as a wind of the Holy Spirit blows upon us. Revival always begins with a repentant heart and God's grace breaking in upon us with reviving life-giving power. God's presence is what revives, restores and rejuvenates our souls.

Begin first by seeking revival so that you can be reformed. It doesn't do any good to reform your ways if you aren't going to seek revival of your spirit. Because then you are doing just to do and not out of a heart filled with God. In this you are held captive by activity for the sake of activity! Isaiah 28:13 says, *"So then, the word of the LORD to them will become: Do and do, do and do, rule on rule, rule on rule; a little here, a little there--so that they will go and fall backward, be injured and snared and captured"*. Want to stay out of the captivity of activity? Seek revival first and then be reformed!

What are some examples of how you have tried to reform your ways without first experiencing revival? Reflect and record your experience in the space below.

Sitting in Isaiah

When we experience revival we are restored to life, consciousness, vigor, and strength, and awakened. When sinners become believers it is a perfect example of God's grace breaking in upon us with reviving power. Revival happens in one life and sometimes in a large group, but it always begins with repentance. God's mission is to renew the whole world, and He begins that work one soul at a time - one broken, bruised, forgotten, drought-stricken, desolate and ruined soul at a time! He begins with *you and me*.

Do you long for revival in your life, family, friends, church or the world? Ask God to begin with you. Start by applying the truths from today's lesson in a conversation with God. Use the space provided to record your prayer.

Optional reading assignment for today: Isaiah Chapter 32.

© Belonging to Him Ministries 2009. All rights reserved.

Sitting in Isaiah

Chapter Six   **Lesson Two**

Read Isaiah 58. **Review** this week's key verse Isaiah 58:8-9a. A look at the original language gives us understanding and insight into the meaning of this passage. Light means illumination, the ability to see and shine. To break forth means to open up or burst forth. The word healing is to restore to soundness or to bring wholeness. Righteousness is to be right, morally, naturally or legally; and also prosperity. The translated word for rear guard is *rereward* and means to cover from behind. Take a moment and consider how your life would look different if every aspect of this verse were true for you.

When we experience His revival we cannot help but experience His reformation. God reforms us by helping us recover His purpose for us and He revives us through showing us how to recover his life in us. He is in the business of renewing tired, worn out, confused and discouraged people. It is what He does best.

To be reformed means to put an end to abuses, disorders and the like, to abandon evil conduct or errors, to correct one's course of action. When God reforms us He awakens in us a new passion and new clarity about what His purpose is for us. When we experience reformation we have a whole new appreciation and love for His truth (His word). This causes a reshaping of our selves and our lives because nothing goes untouched by Him.

The problem addressed in Chapter 58 isn't that the Israelites weren't seeking God or fasting but that they were seeking God and fasting for the wrong reasons. The Israelites were required to fast once a year on the Day of Atonement. While the scriptural word for fasting doesn't describe fasting in detail, the essence is that there is to be some discomfort on that day, which includes self-denial—subduing the flesh to the spirit and repentant sorrow for sins. In Isaiah 58 it is clear that seeking God and fasting wasn't reviving and reforming them, for they were still stuck in the habit of sins. So much so that the Day of Atonement was spent like any other day!

Isaiah lists many sins and offenses of which the Israelites were guilty. Read Isaiah 58 again and make a list of the sins you find listed.

© Belonging to Him Ministries 2009. All rights reserved.

Sitting in Isaiah

Isaiah lists the sins of hypocrisy, self-centeredness, self-serving, disregard for the poor and oppressed, disregard for God and for His standards, harsh judgmental-ness toward others, gossiping, poor stewardship, contempt for others, divisiveness, usury of others for personal gain and pride. It brings another passage of scripture to mind from Proverbs 6:16-19; "There are six things the LORD hates, seven that are detestable to Him; haughty eyes, a lying tongue, hands that shed innocent blood, a heart that devises wicked schemes, feet that are quick to rush into evil, a false witness who pours out lies and a man who stirs up dissension among brothers."

What about you? As we journey through the spiritual spa of Isaiah, I encourage you to look once again at the issue of sin and its supreme importance to God. Spend some moments reflecting on the list above and ask God to reveal any of which you might be guilty. Repent of each sin as God reveals and seek His cleansing, forgiveness and healing from your sins. It helps to keep a record of what God shows you about yourself so that you can review it and remember it. Record your discovery below.

Optional reading assignment for today: Isaiah Chapter 33.

© Belonging to Him Ministries 2009. All rights reserved.

Sitting in Isaiah

Chapter Six   **Lesson Three**

Read all of Isaiah 58 and make a list of God's instructions regarding fasting, both the do's and the don'ts. **Review** this week's key verse Isaiah 58:8-9a by writing it from memory. **Re-read** today's focus verses Isaiah 58:1-8. The word fast means to cover over the mouth. What did God say was wrong with the way they were fasting in verses 1-8?

Fasting means to voluntarily go without food or drink for a period of time. Fasting is seen throughout the Bible as a sign of distress, grief or repentance. Many fast for spiritual renewal and growth, for specific guidance, for healing, for the resolution of problems or for special grace to handle difficult situations. But fasting is always accompanied with prayer for the purpose of getting closer to Father God. (Bright)

There are many healing benefits of fasting as a means of detoxifying and cleansing the body. There are all sorts of medical fasts but the type of fasting I refer to in today's topic is a spiritual fast not for the benefit of the physical body but to benefit the spiritual life. Just as fasting is good for the body it is also very beneficial in aiding the soul to cleanse spiritual toxins. The purpose of refraining from food and favorite beverages, activities and distractions for a set amount of time is to grow deeper in God by clearing away the spiritual toxins and clutter of our hearts and lives.

The problem God had with the fasting the Israelites were doing is that their fasting was with wrong motives, wrong purpose and a wrong heart attitude. While it is good to practice the discipline of fasting it is best to do it in God's way with pure motives, purposes and attitudes.

- Begin by committing to remain private about whether you are fasting, or not. In other words, be careful to not boast to others when you fast.

- Set your objective. Ask yourself why you want to fast. Ask the Holy Spirit to clarify His leading and objectives. This will enable you to pray specifically and strategically.

- Pray about the kind of fast you plan to undertake, i.e. only water and clear liquids, for how long—one meal or several? If you are a beginner start slow with fasting for just one meal before building up to a 1day or even longer fast. I recommend beginning a fast at sundown after enjoying a light evening meal. Avoid carbs right before fasting as they stimulate hunger pangs. Some have certain diseases or medications that prohibit them from fasting from all forms of food. Don't' let your physical condition stop you

© Belonging to Him Ministries 2009. All rights reserved.

Sitting in Isaiah

from reaping the benefits of fasting. You can fast by going on an all liquid diet, which could contain lean protein shakes as a substitute for chewing food. You could build up your fasting muscles by fasting for only one meal, and building up to a longer fasting.

- Decide in advance what type of food and beverages you will avoid and be prepared with the proper foods to support you. You should also pray about what type of activities you will restrict or avoid. If you work outside your home you may decide to fast only on your days off work when you can be near your home. On my fast days I avoid outside contact with others, distractions such as TV or internet access, noise or projects. I limit my activity to light house work, short walks and short necessary errands.

- You should also decide in advance how much time each day you will devote to prayer and scripture reading while on your fast. Plan ahead, by choosing passages of scripture to read in advance that coincide with your purpose of fasting. As an example, if I am fasting for the healing and salvation of another, I study and pray scriptures that apply to that topic when ever I can. Making these decisions and commitments in advance will help you stick to your fast even when distractions and temptations occur. Lastly, when it is time to break your fast, (that is why we call it "breakfast") go slow, beginning with small amounts of food and large amounts of water.

My prayer group and I have set aside one day a week for fasting and prayer. We send out a weekly reminder of our intent along with our requests to one another, but our fasting is generally in private between us and the Lord. We don't go around checking up on each other, but we do encourage each other to persist in the discipline of fasting as it has many spiritual benefits to our spiritual growth. This is precisely why we set an agreed upon day each week to fast. Some of us can't always fast on the same day every week. It isn't about legalism, but about discipline and relationship. While there are many instances in the Bible of corporate fasting, for the most part, fasting is to be private for personal spiritual growth and shouldn't be obvious to others, bragged about or legalistic.

Reflect on what you learned about fasting today and ask God to show you how He wants you to apply these truths to your life. If you feel God calling you to fast, write a prayer of commitment to that end and ask Him to show you what type of fast will be best for you.

© Belonging to Him Ministries 2009. All rights reserved.

Sitting in Isaiah

Optional reading assignment for today: Isaiah Chapter 34.

© Belonging to Him Ministries 2009. All rights reserved.

Sitting in Isaiah

Chapter Six   **Lesson Four**

Read all of Isaiah 58 in your favorite translation. **Review** this week's key verse Isaiah 58:8-9a by saying it out loud. Read today's focus verses Isaiah 58:6-7. What type of fasting has God chosen for us according to verses 6-7? What is fasting suppose to do for you?

Fasting is a way to break the yokes of bondage of sin in our lives and the lives of others. Through fasting and prayer we humble ourselves before God so the Holy Spirit will stir our souls, awaken our churches, and heal our land according to 2 Chronicles 7:14. To experience a meaningful fast it helps to plan a schedule for your self.

Prepare the night before by taking some time to be quiet before the Lord. Use this time in praise and worship and review your scripture passages for the next day. Reading scripture before you fall asleep is always beneficial, but especially during a fast. In the morning begin your day on your knees in praise and worship. Read and meditate on scripture and invite the Holy Spirit to fill you and do His work in you (Philippians 2:13). Pray for God's will to be done in your life and to empower you to be obedient to what ever He calls you to. Willingness to obey is a key to God's speaking directly to you. Playing praise music during your fast may help set the tone and focus your heart.

During the day intersperse light activity and prayer times while minimizing the distractions as much as possible. Allow for concentrated time in listening prayer seeking God's presence

At noon time return to the word and prayer, praying the word back to God. If you are having difficulty concentrating, try taking a short prayer walk. Spend time in intercessory prayer for those in need around you and also for leadership in your community, church and nation. You can choose to break your fast in the late afternoon, with an early evening meal or carry it through to "breakfast".

It just so happens that as I write this lesson I was supposed to be fasting, but circumstances outside of my control (a blinding migraine) have interrupted my plan. As I woke to the headache again today, I felt discouraged that I had somehow failed God because I would have to partake of food in order to take my medication. Satan tried to remind me of what a loser I am, but I managed enough courage to rebuke him. God reminded me of a few things that I want to share with you to encourage you.

© Belonging to Him Ministries 2009. All rights reserved.

Sitting in Isaiah

Fasting is always for us, not for God. Second, God is not legalistic. Thank God for that! One definition of legalism is "salvation by good works". Thank Jesus that He set us free from salvation by works. We are saved by our faith. Thirdly, God reminded me that He looks at my heart and my motives first and that His love for me is so great and never changes! His great compassion for you and me is the same, yesterday, today and forever! And so while today didn't begin like I had planned, it is still redeemable even though it isn't going the way I had hoped. It is His day, so rejoice and be glad!

Is God calling you to reformation? Are there some areas of your life you sense He is asking you to clean up? Write a prayer recording your conversation with Him regarding what you have learned today. If you made a commitment to practice the discipline of fasting, share your decision with a trusted friend who will support you in prayer and perhaps even join you in the effort.

Optional reading assignment for today: Isaiah Chapter 36.

Sitting in Isaiah

Chapter Six   **Lesson Five**

Read Isaiah 58. **Review** this week's key verse Isaiah 58:8-9a. Meditate on today's focus verses 13-14. According to verses 13-14 what is the Sabbath and what are we to do or not do on the Sabbath? What are the benefits God promises to those who keep the Sabbath holy?

Genesis 2:2 is the first time the word Sabbath "Shabbath" (shabbawth) is used and it is the same word used in Isaiah 58:13. It means intermission, to repose, desist from exertion. It refers to the idea of celebrating or a holy day—holiday. In Genesis 2 God rested from His work of creation on the seventh day which had come to be known by the Jews as Saturday. Sunday being the first day of the week has traditionally been the Sabbath in Christianity in commemoration of the resurrection of Christ. The Sabbath is the day which God appointed to be observed by the Jews as a day of rest from all secular labor or employments and to be kept holy and consecrated (set apart) to his service and worship.

The Sabbath is God's gift to us, a day for rest and reflection, a holiday if you will. Part of what devastates, depletes and desolates our soul is a lack of rest and refreshment (which we will talk about in depth in the following chapters). If we kept the Sabbath as a day off from all labor every 6 days, 52 weeks per year then we would have **7½ additional weeks of vacation every year of our lives**! Can you imagine that? Most of us get maybe a week or two of vacation each year, and often unpaid! (Ortlund, p. 392)

God established the Sabbath as a way of protecting us from employers who would over work us and exploit us for their personal and financial gain. The Sabbath was created to help us structure our weeks around honoring God and enjoying one another. Having one day each week where no one is working allows us time to see our families as well as fellowship with other believers. Honoring the Sabbath was God's way of helping to protect us from becoming self-worshiping workaholics overly obsessed with financial gain, productivity, organization and busyness.

When I was growing up in a legalistic denomination we were expected to abide by strict adherence to the Sabbath. On Sundays we weren't to watch TV or take part in any activity that required others to work for our personal enjoyment. All food for Sunday was prepared in advance on Saturday, so that there was little preparation work on Sunday. We typically spent most of the day in fellowship with friends from our church, both new and old, eating, playing games and even taking turns napping in hammocks, under trees, or on a couch or two. I loved Sundays and looked forward to them every week.

© Belonging to Him Ministries 2009. All rights reserved.

Sitting in Isaiah

Years ago in the first year of our marriage, our Pastor Gordon MacDonald of Grace Chapel in Lexington, Massachusetts, gave a sermon on the Sabbath that I have never forgotten. He taught that the Sabbath had 3 purposes: the first to look back over the previous week to re-evaluate and appreciate all God had done and allowed you to do; second, to look up to God, worship, love, praise and appreciate Him for all He has done; and third, to look ahead at the week to come, to pray for wisdom and guidance and to be spiritually prepared for what lay just ahead.

In America the Sabbath is sadly the one holy-day we no longer choose to celebrate. We think by not honoring the Sabbath we are some how freeing ourselves from a religious obligation but in truth we are enslaving ourselves to workaholism. Not honoring the Lord's Day causes us to be unintentionally exploited by our employers, obliterates family intimacy and most of all a loss of an awareness of the sacred. (Ortlund, p. 391)

What has happened to our society since we no longer honor the Sabbath? Are we better off today then we were in previous generations that did keep the Sabbath? Are we freer? Are we happier?

We don't have to accept God's gift of rest from our labor one day a week. We are free to choose. But realize that what ever our choice is, it comes at a cost. Isaiah 58:14 offers a promise to those who choose to honor the Sabbath "to find joy in the Lord, ride on the heights of the land and feast on the inheritance of your father Jacob." The inheritance of Jacob refers to the blessings of the covenant to possess the land (Habakkuk 3:19, Deuteronomy 32:13).

How well do you give yourself rest from all your work? Do you honor the Sabbath? Why or why not? Reflect upon the truth of today's lesson and how God may be asking you to apply this truth to you life. If you are convinced you need to make a change in how you honor the Sabbath, write a prayer of acknowledgement below and ask God for His divine intervention.

Optional reading assignment for today: Isaiah Chapter 37-38.

© Belonging to Him Ministries 2009. All rights reserved.

Sitting in Isaiah

Additional Notes

Sitting in Isaiah

Chapter Seven

Isaiah 5

Sitting in Isaiah

Isaiah 5

I will sing for the one I love a song about his vineyard: My loved one had a vineyard on a fertile hillside. ² He dug it up and cleared it of stones and planted it with the choicest vines. He built a watchtower in it and cut out a winepress as well. Then he looked for a crop of good grapes, but it yielded only bad fruit. ³ "Now you dwellers in Jerusalem and men of Judah, judge between me and my vineyard. ⁴ What more could have been done for my vineyard than I have done for it? When I looked for good grapes, why did it yield only bad? ⁵ Now I will tell you what I am going to do to my vineyard: I will take away its hedge, and it will be destroyed; I will break down its wall, and it will be trampled. ⁶ I will make it a wasteland, neither pruned nor cultivated, and briers and thorns will grow there. I will command the clouds not to rain on it." ⁷ The vineyard of the LORD Almighty is the house of Israel, and the men of Judah are the garden of his delight. And he looked for justice, but saw bloodshed; for righteousness, but heard cries of distress. ⁸ Woe to you who add house to house and join field to field till no space is left and you live alone in the land. ⁹ The LORD Almighty has declared in my hearing: "Surely the great houses will become desolate, the fine mansions left without occupants. ¹⁰ A ten-acre vineyard will produce only a bath of wine, a homer of seed only an ephah of grain." ¹¹ Woe to those who rise early in the morning to run after their drinks, who stay up late at night till they are inflamed with wine. ¹² They have harps and lyres at their banquets, tambourines and flutes and wine, but they have no regard for the deeds of the LORD, no respect for the work of his hands. ¹³ Therefore my people will go into exile for lack of understanding; their men of rank will die of hunger and their masses will be parched with thirst. ¹⁴ Therefore the grave enlarges its appetite and opens its mouth without limit; into it will descend their nobles and masses with all their brawlers and revelers. ¹⁵ So man will be brought low and mankind humbled, the eyes of the arrogant humbled. ¹⁶ But the LORD Almighty will be exalted by his justice, and the holy God will show himself holy by his righteousness. ¹⁷ Then sheep will graze as in their own pasture; lambs will feed among the ruins of the rich. ¹⁸ Woe to those who draw sin along with cords of deceit, and wickedness as with cart ropes, ¹⁹ to those who say, "Let God hurry, let him hasten his work so we may see it. Let it approach, let the plan of the Holy One of Israel come, so we may know it." ²⁰ Woe to those who call evil good and good evil, who put darkness for light and light for darkness, who put bitter for sweet and sweet for bitter. ²¹ Woe to those who are wise in their own eyes and clever in their own sight. ²² Woe to those who are heroes at drinking wine and champions at mixing drinks, ²³ who acquit the guilty for a bribe, but deny justice to the innocent. ²⁴ Therefore, as tongues of fire lick up straw and as dry grass sinks down in the flames, so their roots will decay and their flowers blow away like dust; for they have rejected the law of the LORD Almighty and spurned the word of the Holy One of Israel. ²⁵ Therefore the LORD's anger burns against his people; his hand is raised and he strikes them down. The mountains shake, and the dead bodies are like refuse in the streets. Yet for all this, his anger is not turned away, his hand is still upraised. ²⁶ He lifts up a banner for the distant nations, he whistles for those at the ends of the earth. Here they come, swiftly and speedily! ²⁷ Not one of them grows tired or stumbles, not one slumbers or sleeps; not a belt is loosened at the waist, not a sandal thong is broken. ²⁸ Their arrows are sharp, all their bows are strung; their horses' hoofs seem like flint, their chariot wheels like a whirlwind. ²⁹ Their roar is like that of the lion, they roar like young lions; they growl as they seize their prey and carry it off with no one to rescue. ³⁰ In that day they will roar over it like the roaring of the sea. And if one looks at the land, he will see darkness and distress; even the light will be darkened by the clouds.

(NIV)

© Belonging to Him Ministries 2009. All rights reserved.

Sitting in Isaiah

Chapter Seven **Lesson One**

Read Isaiah 5. **Key Verse** Isaiah 5:20-21 "Woe to those who call evil good and good evil, who put darkness for light and light for darkness, who put bitter for sweet and sweet for bitter. Woe to those who are wise in their own eyes and clever in their own sight." **Review** this week's key verse and write it on an index card to carry with you to review throughout the day and week.

Isaiah chapter 5 begins as a parable. A parable is a way to represent or explain a truth through a fable or by fiction. Isaiah 5:7 explains that the vineyard planted represents Israel. God, the owner of the vineyard and gardener gave them every advantage to insure that they would be strong and produce a bounty of prime healthy fruit. Instead of a bountiful harvest, Israel produced bad fruit, but not just any old bad fruit. We know from the Hebrew text that it is *poisoned fruit* from the word *be'ushiym* (be-oo-sheem') which means *poisoned berries*.

The poisoned fruit they produced were their sins which are listed and distinguished by six "*woes*". A woe is like a threat or warning to indicate that somebody is going to regret something. Skim over Isaiah 5 again looking for the word "woe" and make a list of them below.

Our journey through the Spiritual Spa takes us to an essential part of spiritual health and wellness and it is what I call Spiritual Exfoliation of the Soul. Exfoliation means separation and is the removal of the surface of something either by peeling off in thin layers or scaling off in large chunks. The work of spiritual exfoliation is done through abiding in the Spirit, as we become willing participants to allow God to slough off the dead flesh on us. The process is typically uncomfortable and sometimes downright painful! It is never easy and takes work to allow God to peel away the layers of our hearts so that we are cleansed of the dead flesh and able to bear good fruit. The work can be unpleasant, at times inconvenient and hard, but the rewards and benefits far outweigh the costs! "No pain, no gain" is really true! The end result is the beauty of being completely renovated, restored and rejuvenated.

© Belonging to Him Ministries 2009. All rights reserved.

Sitting in Isaiah

Isaiah 5 is God's call to each one of us to be holy, separating ourselves from evil. When we come to Christ, accepting Him as both our Savior and our Lord we are agreeing to live differently. We are acknowledging that the way we were living up to the point of our salvation hasn't been working for us, and that we need a change. God wants us to have all of His abundant blessings and be free. Our freedom comes through submission. Odd when you think about it, but so true. This translates into cleaning up our lives through the work of spiritual exfoliation of the sin nature.

We all have a sin nature since our conception—we were born with it (Psalm 51:5). "The sin nature is the capacity and inclination to do those things that in no way commend us to God" (Ryrie, p. 1948). Paul describes the acts of the sin nature in Galatians 5: 19-21, made more poignant from The Message:

"It is obvious what kind of life develops out of trying to get your own way all the time: repetitive, loveless, cheap sex; a stinking accumulation of mental and emotional garbage; frenzied and joyless grabs for happiness; trinket gods; magic-show religion; paranoid loneliness; cutthroat competition; all-consuming-yet-never-satisfied wants; a brutal temper; an impotence to love or be loved; divided homes and divided lives; small-minded and lopsided pursuits; the vicious habit of depersonalizing everyone into a rival; uncontrolled and uncontrollable addictions; ugly parodies of community.

Make a list below of the actions of the sin nature in your own words. Are there any in particular that you struggle against?

© Belonging to Him Ministries 2009. All rights reserved.

Sitting in Isaiah

Write a prayer of confession for the acts of the sin nature God has revealed that you need to overcome. If you realize you may have a stronghold in one or more of these acts listed above, I urge you to return to Chapter 5, Lesson One of our study and take the steps recommended to begin to tear down your strongholds.

Optional reading assignment for today: Isaiah Chapter 39.

Sitting in Isaiah

Chapter Seven　　　　　　　　　　　　　　　　　　　　　　　　　　　　**Lesson Two**

Read Isaiah 5. **Review** this week's key verse Isaiah 5:21-20. Contemplate the meaning of the key verse. What does it mean for evil to be declared as good and good as evil? Recall a time when you might have witnessed this happening. Have you ever seen someone substituting light for darkness and darkness for light? Would you call this deception? Record your example of this below.

Veronica knows all about deception. She was an honor student at a prominent Ivy League University when she joined a church fellowship that was active on her college campus. There she and her husband met, married and raised their children in this church. The church leaders *required* them to give up large portions of their income, allow homeless to live with them and devote all their talent and free time to serving, night and day. They ran themselves into complete exhaustion and before long both Veronica and her husband were medically treated with anti-depressants to combat the darkness that had overcome them. Eventually the pressures of being members of this church became too much for their marriage and it ended in divorce. Condemned by their church family for their divorce, they both sought help outside of their church. While undergoing counseling they discovered the shocking truth that their fellowship was actually a well-known cult, and they had been living, supporting and believing innumerable lies for 17 years! The untold grief Veronica, her ex-husband and children experienced was incredible. They had been deceived, and the deceivers had stolen their faith, their health, their happiness, their marriage and their family. Even now, years later, the wreckage and carnage remain. Veronica, her children and ex struggle to know, understand and believe the truth of who God is, without doubts or suspicions.

Do you know someone who is currently under a veil of deception? Take a few moments to write a prayer for them, and countless others like them, asking God to reveal His truth to them and to be set free from their darkness.

Beloved, we need to take the greatest care to see that we ourselves are not deceived! We live in a dark world, and Satan is the father of lies! He comes as an angel of light, (2 Corinthians 11:14) seeking to deceive you and yours. His goal is to get you to believe his

© Belonging to Him Ministries 2009. All rights reserved.

Sitting in Isaiah

lies! God gives us His truth and His Spirit as a plumb line for living. We must be certain that every part of our lives lines up with the Word of God.

The world hates what is good—because it hates God. We must guard our hearts from reading, watching and believing that evil is somehow good and good is evil. The world argues against good, runs it down and condemns it, poke's fun at it, makes jokes about it and persecutes any one brave enough to take a stand for Godly virtues. The world is proud of evil and promotes, justifies, applauds, and even recommends it.

There is no more certain path to drought, devastation and deprivation of life-giving nutrients for our souls than relying on ourselves apart from the Word of God to supply our hearts and minds with what we perceive to be true. We go looking to the world to give us wisdom, understanding, information and opinion on how we are to live life. We shop for truth like we shop for a new car, a new restaurant or a life mate! We are living light years ahead of ourselves, with more information than we can possibly absorb at the stroke of our computer key board. It is dangerous for believers to look to the world for help. Even Solomon understood this when he wrote Proverbs 3:5-6 "Trust in the LORD with all your heart and lean not on your own understanding; in all your ways acknowledge him, and he will make your paths straight."

Where or what do you turn to when you have a problem, are sad, confused, lonely, unsure or undecided? Is your first impulse to turn to a trusted friend or spouse, pastor, a popular book, the internet, Dr. Oz, Dr. Phil, Dr. Spock, Oprah or your mother? Do you rely on yourself, Google, books, magazines or TV to be your first responder? It isn't that these sources are necessarily bad, (though I would argue that if ungodly they are a bad source of help and information) but if they are your first source of wisdom—your first responders, then you are in trouble whether you realize it yet, or not.

Sitting in Isaiah

If we aren't turning *to* God *first* for everything and anything we face then we are turning *from* Him! Write a prayer today asking Him to help you learn to trust Him more and look to Him first for His counsel and advice for living.

Optional reading assignment for today: Isaiah Chapter 41.

Sitting in Isaiah

Chapter Seven   **Lesson Three**

Read all of Isaiah 5 in your favorite translation and look for the poor choices that caused Israel to fall into desolation and ruin, record your findings below. **Review** this week's key verse Isaiah 5:20-21 by writing it from memory.

We are all born with a sin nature. It's the bend in us that is selfishly self-centered; we want our own way, want everything to be all about us, we want what we want when we want it and leave no room for the word "no". Our sin nature is our *flesh*. It is the "earthly part of man, representing lusts and desires (Ephesians 2:3). The flesh is contrary to the Spirit (Galatians 5:17) and therefore cannot please God (Romans 8:8)" (Lockyer et al.). Our struggle to live free, clean, restored, fulfilled and refreshed hinges on only *one choice*: to walk in the spirit or walk in the flesh. It sounds so simple, but yet is hard to do because it comes down to the long and sometimes lonely walk of obedience.

We are the only ones who can put our flesh to death and keep it dead with the Lord's help. "Being dead to sin doesn't mean that our 'old self' no longer exists, but that is has been separated from our new and true self. In our innermost being we've been disconnected from sin, divorced from it. Sin is no longer our true nature and we no longer need to submit to its mastery" (Myers, *Christ Life*, p. 93). Our daily gritting-our-teeth-mantra "death to my flesh" should instead claim with gratitude "death to flesh…alive to God! The old me has died and the new me is alive" (Romans 6:4, 6). [This is not simply a matter of grasping a hard concept, but of continually choosing to remind ourselves and rely upon the truths that we have died to sin and we have risen to God.] "Together these two truths about sin cancel our old relationship with sin and death and inaugurate our new relationship with God" (Myers, *Christ Life*, p. 89).

At times we must rely on the fact that God says this is true of us, even if we don't understand it or even realize it yet. Why is it so important for us to understand these truths? Record your answers below and write a prayer telling the Lord how you personally accept these facts, what they mean to you and how this knowledge will change your life.

© Belonging to Him Ministries 2009. All rights reserved.

Sitting in Isaiah

Write a brief truth statement from today's lesson to use day by day, hour by hour if needed.

"Pause and take time to worship the Lord today by glorying in the cross of our Lord Jesus Christ. In His presence, reflect on what His death has meant in your relationship to sin." (Myers, *Christ Life*, p. 88) Record your holy conversation below.

Optional reading assignment for today: Isaiah Chapter 42.

© Belonging to Him Ministries 2009. All rights reserved.

Sitting in Isaiah

Chapter Seven   **Lesson Four**

Read all of Isaiah 5 in your favorite translation. **Review** this week's key verse Isaiah 5: 20-21 by saying it out loud. What verses from Isaiah 5 catch your attention and cause you to rethink some of your values? From verse 24 what does God say will happen to those who reject and spurn His word?

We are in a constant spiritual battle—the war between the flesh and the spirit. This battle actually begins and ends in our mind. Whether our selfish self-centered flesh struggle is over food, anger, spending, sex, gossip, laziness, low self-esteem, anger or addiction, it all begins in our mind. Typically it begins when we see something that triggers the idea, and then we allow the thought to take hold. Soon we are off searching for a way to fulfill the desire of our flesh. But really we can trace it back to one simple thing: a thought. Proverbs 23:7 says as we think in our heart, so are we!

In her book *Battlefield of the Mind,* Joyce Meyer discuses the mentality that kept the children of Israel traveling for forty years on what should have been an eleven day journey (p. 185)! They kept going around and around the same mountain rather than moving on, because they had a wilderness mentality. What about you? Do you sometimes struggle with a mental outlook that is weak, defeated, self-pitying, blaming, shaming, lazy and irresponsible? Do you get stuck in your devastation and find yourself unable to move forward into renovation? Record your insights below.

Sitting in Isaiah

Joyce lists ten "wilderness mentalities"; lies that the children of Israel allowed themselves to believe. Here are a few for our study today to help us understand that the war between our flesh and our spirit is begun and won in our mind!

Wilderness Mentality:
- My future is determined by my past and my present.
- Please make everything easy; I can't take it if things are too hard.
- Don't make me wait for anything; I deserve everything immediately.
- My life is so miserable; I feel sorry for myself because my life is so wretched!
- Why shouldn't I be envious and jealous when everybody is better off than I am?
- I'm going to do it my way; or not at all (Meyer, pp. 185-278)

Do you relate to any of these? If so which ones and why?

It isn't our circumstances that need to change; it's our heart's attitude! We need to pay close attention to our thought life and have our minds renewed by the word of God. There are many unconscious thoughts that we think about. Tapes of hurtful conversations and negative self-talk playing over and over in our heads. David understood this problem well. He prayed for truth and wisdom in his innermost being—the sub-conscious place where thoughts often go undetected by the conscious mind (Psalm 51:6).

Begin today with a new fresh approach. Ask God to anoint your mind with the Holy Spirit. Set Him as the security guard of your mind to alert you when negative or sinful thoughts are born. Apply the word of God through meditation and prayer. Use scripture to replace wrong thoughts. You cannot simply stop thinking a wrong thought, you must replace it with a right thought from God's word! It's important for us to understand that we really aren't supposed to listen to ourselves, that is we should listen through the ears of the Spirit so that we understand what we are thinking, but we shouldn't believe everything we think about! We spend our entire lives in our own personal mental universe! We should do everything we can to ensure that the quality of our mental world is one that cultivates peace, faith, hope, joy and love. This can only be achieved through the power of the Holy Spirit in us together with the Word of God.

© Belonging to Him Ministries 2009. All rights reserved.

Sitting in Isaiah

What truth from today's lesson are you in need of experiencing in your life? What part of the formula for Godly thoughts do you need to ramp up to insure your personal mental universe is one that is pleasing to God? Write your answers by way of a prayer, asking God to fill you with His Spirit and renew your mind.

Optional reading assignment for today: Isaiah Chapter 44.

© Belonging to Him Ministries 2009. All rights reserved.

Sitting in Isaiah

Chapter Seven   **Lesson Five**

Read Isaiah 5 out loud. **Review** this week's key verse from memory, Isaiah 58:8-9a. Review verses 1-7 and notice all God did for the vineyard (some of it is detected by what he stopped doing). In what ways did God show His presence, provision and protection over the vineyard (Israel)?

Throughout scripture God's people are depicted as a vineyard, or planting of the Lord. The parable of the vineyard in Isaiah 5 is a powerful picture of how much God loves us and all He has done for us to insure we grow healthy and strong, producing a bountiful harvest. The metaphors in this parable are applicable to us as we journey through our spiritual spa and worth our time today to look at what God did for the vineyard as what He has done for us.

Isaiah 5:1: God selected the choicest land for his vineyard of fertile soil rich in essential nutrients to feed the plants and in the perfect location for optimal growth.

Application: God has placed you exactly where He wants you. He pre-determined for you to be born into your family and even where you are to live and placed you where you are for optimal growth. He planned your location, it wasn't some random selection. How does knowing this truth change the way you view your current life position?

Isaiah 5:2: God dug up or loosened the soil to aerate and allow for drainage.

Application: God prepared the place where you are in advance of our arrival, so that it would be just right for you. How does knowing this truth change the way you view your current life position?

© Belonging to Him Ministries 2009. All rights reserved.

Sitting in Isaiah

Isaiah 5:2: He cleared the soil of rocks and stones which prohibit the roots from going down deep and from choking out the roots from gaining access to essential nutrients.

Application: He is in the business of removing obstacles so that you can grow and nothing is too hard for Him. Your walls are ever before Him….Is 49:16. He knows what is in your way and will remove it at the appropriate time. How does knowing this truth offer you hope given the current obstacles you are facing today? List those obstacles and ask Him for His help in removing them.

Isaiah 5:2: He chose the very best, the "choicest" vines to plant.

Application: God is a quality God. He doesn't go for cheap stuff, cheap imitations. He makes and gives the very best. You are the cream of the crop! The very best of God! How does knowing this truth change the way you view yourself and your value to God?

© Belonging to Him Ministries 2009. All rights reserved.

Sitting in Isaiah

Isaiah 5:2: He built a watchtower in order to be able to watch over the vineyard, to protect it from invaders and also to lodge within His vineyard as a way of coexisting with His vines and enjoying them as He watched them grow.

Application: God is always watching over us and our safety is a high priority to Him. God is present with us by choice and loves being around us to enjoy watching us grow. How should I apply this truth to my relationship with Him?

Isaiah 5:2: He put a winepress within as an altar where sacrifices, the fruits of the vineyards would be brought to Him.

Application: We have to die to ourselves to really live. We are a living sacrifice. How does knowing this truth change the way I live day to day?

Isaiah 5:5: He put a hedge, a wall and a gate to protect us from our enemies.

Application: Take our enemies seriously because He does. How might I apply this understanding according to what I have learned in this study regarding the evil one?

© Belonging to Him Ministries 2009. All rights reserved.

Sitting in Isaiah

Isaiah 5:6: He prunes to help the vines produce better fruit.

Application: Pruning is essential to the vine having good health and producing large amounts of fruit (John 15) Allow God the freedom as the Gardener of your life, to cut away those branches that need to be removed. Have you experienced His pruning work in your life? If so, please explain.

Isaiah 5:6: He cultivated the ground to keep out the weeds, briers and thorns.

Application: Give God access to your life and the freedom to weed out those things that might harm you, block your progress or overtake you. Have you experienced God weeding your garden? What things has He removed that you may have had difficulty relinquishing? Has He weeded out things you were happy to see go? Ask Him to continue to weed out the weeds in your life.

© Belonging to Him Ministries 2009. All rights reserved.

Sitting in Isaiah

Isaiah 5:6: He commanded the clouds to rain on it to provide the appropriate amount of water needed for perfect growing conditions.

Application: God knows how much rain you need, and more importantly how much rain you can take. Accept the rain He gives and give Him thanks for it. Trust Him to supply all you need according to the riches in Christ Jesus. In what ways have you questioned God because you felt you had too little or too much of something in your life?

Optional reading assignment for today: Isaiah Chapter 45.

© Belonging to Him Ministries 2009. All rights reserved.

Chapter Eight

Isaiah 55

Sitting in Isaiah

Isaiah 55

¹ "Come, all you who are thirsty, come to the waters and you who have no money, come, buy and eat! Come, buy wine and milk without money and without cost. ² Why spend money on what is not bread, and your labor on what does not satisfy? Listen, listen to me, and eat what is good, and your soul will delight in the richest of fare ³ Give ear and come to me; hear me, that your soul may live. I will make an everlasting covenant with you, my faithful love promised to David. ⁴ See, I have made him a witness to the peoples, a leader and commander of the peoples. ⁵ Surely you will summon nations you know not, and nations that do not know you will hasten to you, because of the LORD your God, the Holy One of Israel, for he has endowed you with splendor." ⁶ Seek the LORD while he may be found; call on him while he is near. ⁷ Let the wicked forsake his way and the evil man his thoughts. Let him turn to the LORD, and he will have mercy on him, and to our God, for he will freely pardon. ⁸ "For my thoughts are not your thoughts, neither are your ways my ways," declares the LORD. ⁹ "As the heavens are higher than the earth, so are my ways higher than your ways and my thoughts than your thoughts. ¹⁰ As the rain and the snow come down from heaven, and do not return to it without watering the earth and making it bud and flourish, so that it yields seed for the sower and bread for the eater, ¹¹ so is my word that goes out from my mouth: It will not return to me empty, but will accomplish what I desire and achieve the purpose for which I sent it. ¹² You will go out in joy and be led forth in peace; the mountains and hills will burst into song before you, and all the trees of the field will clap their hands. ¹³ Instead of the thorn bush will grow the pine tree, and instead of briers the myrtle will grow. This will be for the LORD's renown, for an everlasting sign, which will not be destroyed."

(NIV)

Sitting in Isaiah

Chapter Eight   **Lesson One**

Read Isaiah 55. **Key Verse** Isaiah 55:11-12a "So is my word that goes out from my mouth: It will not return to me empty, but will accomplish what I desire and achieve the purpose for which I sent it. You will go out in joy and be led forth in peace." **Review** this week's key verse and write it on an index card to carry with you to review throughout the day and week. As you review the verse think of an example when you have witnessed the power of God's Word. Record your reflection below.

An essential part of soul renovation is moisture. Our soul needs hydration just as our bodies need to be hydrated consistently to be healthy. The Word of God is moisture to our soul. It protects us from becoming diseased, dry, barren and desolate. The water of the Word heals, restores and gives life (Isaiah 55:10).

Luke 5 reveals the power of the Word as we meet a man who terrorized an entire town. He was demon possessed, meaning a demon had invaded his body. In this case he had multiple demons, literally a legion of demons (meaning many) were living in him. Everything man could do had been done to help this poor guy. He ran around naked, cutting himself with stones and brutalizing himself. No one could contain him even with heavy shackles and chains which he could break apart with super-human strength. He was a crazed maniac, living among the dead in the tombs up in the hills outside of town. He spent his nights terrorizing the neighboring towns and villages with his cries of terror and screaming fits of rage echoing through the countryside. Jesus had to come through a storm for him—Satan's weak attempt to keep Jesus away! By His word, the demons fled. Talk about "swine flew"! The demons were hurled into a pack of pigs, and the "swine flew" down the hill and over the edge into the sea below! The whole town was so intrigued they came out to see for themselves! What they found was astonishing! Not the part about the "swine flew", but the part about the crazy man! He was dressed, sitting with Jesus and in his right mind! They were so frightened by the presence and power of Jesus that they urged him to leave! Some thanks, I say!

The story from Luke 5 is an example of the incredible healing power of the word of God. The same power that raised Jesus from the dead healed this man. This same power is available to us not only through His Holy Spirit living in us but also living in the Word of God. In Luke 5 we witness the power of the presence and words of Jesus which restored the man spiritually, as

© Belonging to Him Ministries 2009. All rights reserved.

Sitting in Isaiah

he sat with Jesus, physically as Jesus put clothes on him and emotionally/mentally as he was finally "in his right mind".

God's Word is the key nutrient in hydrating our souls for health and wholeness. He wants us to partake of Him through His Word, believe it so much that it becomes part of our prayers to Him and thereby transforms our lives from the inside out. His desire is for us to be healed, refreshed, renewed and completely restored through the power of His Word. To be transformed by the renewing of our mind through the washing of the Word. Our key verse for this week is an exhortation to do just that.

What areas of your life are you asking God to restore? Ask Him to speak the truth of His Word into specific areas of your life that need His renovating work.

Do you drink in the life giving water of the Word consistently or is your soul suffering from dehydration? Do you take God at His word, believe it, pray it and then live it accordingly? If you struggle to do this, ask God to help you have the desire and discipline. He does not want you to stay in your desolate desert forever! He wants to bring you out in joy and lead you forward in peace! He is willing and more than able to heal and restore you. Trust in Him and in the power of His Word.

Optional reading assignment for today: Isaiah Chapter 46.

© Belonging to Him Ministries 2009. All rights reserved.

Sitting in Isaiah

Chapter Eight   **Lesson Two**

Read Isaiah 55 out loud. **Review** this week's key verse Isaiah 55:11-12a. Read today's focus verses Isaiah 55:8-13 and reflect on how God speaks to you.

The use of the word *"word"* in verse 11 is *dabar* (daw-baw) which means to speak a word or a matter. The first use of the word *Dabar* appears in Genesis 15:1 "The word (*dabar*) from the Lord came to Abram in a vision." God's first words to him were: "Do not be afraid, Abram. I am your shield, your very great reward."

Write Genesis 15:1 below inserting your name.

God speaks to us through His indwelling Holy Spirit (John 14:26), His Word (Isaiah 55:11), through nature (Romans 1:20), and through other believers, signs and miracles (Romans 15:18). One of the most common ways we can hear God speak to us is from His Word. God's word is so powerful everything we see, touch, feel and experience is held together by the power of the Word (Hebrews 1:3). Hear how powerful the word is from Hebrews 4:12 of *The Message*. "God means what he says. What he says goes. His powerful Word is sharp as a surgeon's scalpel, cutting through everything, whether doubt or defense, laying us open to listen and obey. Nothing and no one is impervious to God's Word. We can't get away from it—no matter what."

God still speaks the way He spoke to the Israelites in emotional word pictures. This is a method of communicating a powerful message in a way that moves the hearer emotionally to have a connection. For example, since the Israelites lived in a land dependent completely upon rainfall for giving it life and vitality they certainly comprehended the analogy God gave them in Isaiah 55:1 and 10-11 where He referred to them being thirsty and needing rainfall. God wants to make a connection with us, so He speaks to us in ways that we can relate to so that we "hear" Him.

Often people complain that they are frustrated with God because they don't hear Him speak to them. If this is your concern then my question is, are you in the Word? Do you regularly read, meditate and memorize His Word? If not then it means you really don't love His Word and therefore severely restrict your ability to hear God speak.

© Belonging to Him Ministries 2009. All rights reserved.

Sitting in Isaiah

To be transformed, changed, renovated and restored we must be in the Word. We can't just read it, but we have to do what it says (James 1:22). To be able to apply the Word we have to know the Word. To know the Word we have to meditate and memorize it.

Meditating on and memorizing scripture can be much easier if you follow these guidelines.

- Pick a verse that has meaning to you, preferably something you read in your quiet time or Bible study that connected with you.

- Don't demand word-perfect-memorization from yourself.

- Meditate on the verse initially before trying to memorize it.

- Begin by visualizing the verse in its context (read the verses before and after) and apply its truth to your life.

- Write it a few times in your spiritual growth journal, put it on an index card (or two) and place it in a prominent place where you will see it throughout your day.

- Focus on memorizing the address, or *reference* of the verse and memorize the *truth* of the verse in your own words.

- Pray the verse back to God and review it several times a day.

- Share the verse with a friend or two.

What things from the list above are hard for you to follow through on? Ask God to help you be more disciplined in applying His Word to your life.

What God has already said in His Word is enough and complete, and yet often we want God to say something new to us. If this is true for you, go back to what He has already told you and apply those truths to your life. If sometimes you lack the desire to live and love the Word, ask God to bless you with a new deep desire and hunger for His Word. God always answers prayers that bring you closer to Him! Record your prayer below.

Optional reading assignment for today: Isaiah Chapter 47.

© Belonging to Him Ministries 2009. All rights reserved.

Sitting in Isaiah

Chapter Eight   Lesson Three

Read all of Isaiah 55 in your favorite translation and **review** this week's key verse Isaiah 55:11-12a by writing it from memory. Read today's focus verses 55:1-3. Think about what it feels like when you are completely satisfied (verse 2). *Satisfied*—to do or offer enough to make someone feel pleased or content, to fulfill a need or gratify a desire. To be *content* is to be quietly satisfied and happy, ready and willing to accept a situation or comply with a proposed course of action. What is God offering that promises to completely satisfy in verses 1-3?

We have insatiable appetites and it's not in our nature to ever be satisfied or content. Our condition is compounded by the fact that our world bombards us with conscious and unconscious messages that we need more than we already have and that in and of ourselves we don't quite measure up. Every day we hear suggestions that may not be pretty enough, thin enough, beautiful enough, loved enough, smart enough, successful enough, rich enough. The list is endless.

Do you sometimes feel like you are "not enough" in a particular area of your life? Record those areas in which you feel inadequate. What are some of the things that you do so that you will feel like you are meeting expectations? Explain below.

God created us to have needs and wants and we weren't ever expected to be perfect apart from God filling us. We were created with a God-shaped vacuum in our souls and the only thing that can fill that hole is Him. Instead of looking to find our satisfaction in Him we fill up on cheap substitutes that will never satisfy (Isaiah 55:2). In what kind of worldly things do we look for satisfaction?

© Belonging to Him Ministries 2009. All rights reserved.

Sitting in Isaiah

The satisfaction the world offers us is costly. But according to Isaiah 55 what fills, satisfies and satiates our souls is FREE. Remember the phrase "the best things in life are free"? Well, it is true! What really fills us up, costs us nothing, but it cost God His Son Jesus everything. He freely gave His life so that we can live in God's presence. God sent His Holy Spirit to us so that we can be filled up with God's presence and know complete satisfaction in Him. We receive God's gift of His Holy Spirit at our moment of conversion when we believe and accept Jesus as our Savior (2 Corinthians 1:22; Ephesians 1:13). God's Spirit is always with believers, but the degree to which we have the fullness of God is dependent upon us. Being filled with God, (His Spirit) is our own responsibility, and it is vital that we understand that to not seek His fullness of the Spirit is a sin (Ephesians 5:18). We can have the fullness of the Spirit simply by asking. Prayer, praise, reading the Word, being obedient, fellowshipping with other believers, sharing Christ and using our spiritual gifting all impact how much we are filled.

God's Holy Spirit has many roles to fill. He is the third person of the Trinity and exercises the power of the Father and the Son in creation and redemption. He is the power by which believers come to Christ (John 6:63) and see with new eyes of faith and He is closer to us than we are to ourselves. The Holy Spirit is our teacher (1 Corinthians 2:9-15), helper/counselor (John 14:26) and comforter (2 Corinthians 1:4). He is God's seal upon us (2 Corinthians 1:22), interceding for us (Romans 8:26) and always brings glory to the Father and the Son (John 8). The Holy Spirit anoints believers with gifts (1 Corinthians 12) and Godly attributes (Galatians 5:22).

What role of the Holy Spirit are you most in need of in your life today? Write your answer by way of a prayer below seeking His filling and expressing the needs of your heart. End your prayer time in praise and thanksgiving to God to bring you closer to Him.

Optional reading assignment for today: Isaiah Chapter 48 and 49.

© Belonging to Him Ministries 2009. All rights reserved.

Sitting in Isaiah

Chapter Eight   **Lesson Four**

Read all of Isaiah 55 from your favorite translation. **Review** this week's key verse Isaiah 55:11-12a by saying it out loud from memory. Review today's focus verses, Isaiah 55:1-3 and think about all the things that we do in order to fill ourselves up, so that we will feel content and satisfied.

Susan has been in a difficult marriage for more than 17 years. She is a strong believer but her husband isn't certain about what he believes. Though Susan had grounds to leave him years ago, she stayed with him for the sake of their children and out of obedience to God. Her husband Tim has never been one to give positive attention to Susan, to express love to her or to build her up. He is a narcissistic person and his world has always revolved around himself. Now that Tim's body is overtaken with cancer, he is more selfish and self-centered than ever. Everyday it is a struggle for Susan to show Christ-like love toward someone who isn't loving or giving in return. Tim is a taker. Caring for her terminally ill husband and children while trying to work and provide for the family means that Susan is nearly always running on empty.

Susan's difficult situation might be unique to us, but the lessons God has taught her along the way are essential for our own spiritual health. God made us with three tanks that need to be filled for us to live refreshed, renewed, restored lives. Our spiritual tank we discussed yesterday and how it is our responsibility to be filled up to the fullness of God. We also are responsible to keep our emotional and physical tanks filled. It is important for us to understand that *we are empty vessels and so we will always be filled with something*. Whether we fill up on junk and stuff that can never satisfy or we fill up on what really satisfies, is up to us.

God wants us to understand five truths to help us to be vessels that are filled and able to pour out when appropriate.

- *To know what we need in order to be filled (and distinguish between needs and wants).*

- *To know when we need to be refilled*

- *To knowing what depletes us.*

- *To make a plan for getting refilled*

- *To ask for help getting refilled when needed.*

It is a challenge to stay on plan and get our self refilled when we know we are running on empty. It is easy to allow other seemingly more important things to get in the way or guilt ourselves out of doing what we know we need to do, and so we play the victim. Many of us struggle to take care of ourselves because we are what I call *Victim-vendors*. A *Victim-Vendor* dispenses the feeling of helplessness to everyone around her. She feels duped, taken advantage of and powerless to help herself. She blames her empty tanks on everyone who takes from her, and takes no responsibility for herself to be filled.

© Belonging to Him Ministries 2009. All rights reserved.

Sitting in Isaiah

Do you struggle with being a victim-vendor or do you know victim-vendors who expect too much from you? Record your insights below.

It is hard to learn to ask for what we need in order to be refilled. Many believe the lie that says "significant others in our life are supposed to know what we need, when we need it and fill us up accordingly, without our ever having to ask". It's just not true. The only person who can read our mind is God. We need to relieve this unfair burden we have placed on our friends and loved ones to perform for us and make us feel better. While it is idyllic and even Christ-like when our friends and family go out of their way (without our every asking them to) to make a deposit in our emotional tank, we shouldn't be placing the sole burden of our being filled to capacity on them.

Are you able to ask for what you need when you need it from both people and God? If not, why not? Reflect on what you need in order to be filled, not what you want. Ask the Spirit to show you the difference and write a prayer telling God of your needs

It can be hard to admit our weaknesses and vulnerabilities, especially if we don't feel safe in relationships. Do you have people in your life who show their love and value of you in tangible ways that fill your tank and satisfy you? If so, write a prayer thanking God for

Sitting in Isaiah

them. If not, ask God to bring them into your life and to meet your need in some other tangible way in the meantime.

What fills you? Remember that most things that really fill us are free. It might cost a little to get yourself to the ocean for a walk on the beach, or a pair of walking shoes so that you can hike more comfortably, but the actual activity is free and the satisfaction is completely fulfilling. Make three columns and list those things that fill you up physically, emotionally and spiritually. Consider your needs (not your wants), choose wisely, make a plan and ask if you need help. God has already given you everything you need for life and Godliness (2 Peter 1:3).

Optional reading assignment for today: Isaiah Chapter 50.

© Belonging to Him Ministries 2009. All rights reserved.

Sitting in Isaiah

Chapter Eight   **Lesson Five**

Read Isaiah 55 out loud. **Review** this week's key verse from memory, Isaiah 55:11-12a. One powerful way we can apply Isaiah 55:11 and experience the power of the Word and the presence of God is by praying His Word back to Him. Here is an example of how this can be done using Isaiah 55. Be blessed by the Word today and pray this prayer with me.

"Oh Lord, thank you for calling me and inviting me to come to You. I come to You because I am thirsty and hungry for life giving nutrients that will fill me and satisfy me. I am weary of striving to fill up on junk that leaves me empty and dissatisfied, even more hungry. How grateful I am that what You offer me is free. All I need to do is believe. I am grateful that You have made the same covenant with me that you made with David, to be loved and set apart by You for your glory, that many will see You glorified through me. I pray for those who do not know you to seek You while there is still time. I pray especially for ... (insert names). Soften their hearts through the conviction of the Holy Spirit to turn away from evil and turn to You. God, I am in awe of your plan of redemption. It is nearly incomprehensible to me that You can and will forgive anyone who asks. I cannot imagine Your thoughts oh God. For You are God, and Your thoughts are so much bigger, higher and holier than mine ever can be! Because You are such a big God, You have ways of doing things that I often don't understand or appreciate. How thankful I am for You and the power of what You say. For Your words have permeated my soul. They have brought the rain into my life to make my soul like a beautiful garden. The power of Your Word has healed me, restored me and set me on a new pathway. I am humbled to know that whatever You say is accomplished and I take courage, comfort and hope in the knowledge that You always do what You say You will do. When I take in your Word it brings joy and peace to my parched soul. Your word protects my soul from weeds overtaking it and nourishes me so that I grow tall and strong in You. What a blessing to know that my growth will be a sign for others as evidence of Your greatness! Make my life a monument of Your glory and greatness of God!

Amen

Optional reading assignment for today: Isaiah Chapter 51 and 52.

© Belonging to Him Ministries 2009. All rights reserved.

Chapter Nine

Isaiah 62

Sitting in Isaiah

Isaiah 62

For Zion's sake I will not keep silent, for Jerusalem's sake I will not remain quiet, till her righteousness shines out like the dawn, her salvation like a blazing torch. ² The nations will see your righteousness, and all kings your glory; you will be called by a new name that the mouth of the LORD will bestow. ³ You will be a crown of splendor in the LORD's hand, a royal diadem in the hand of your God. ⁴ No longer will they call you Deserted, or name your land Desolate. But you will be called Hephzibah, and your land Beulah; for the LORD will take delight in you, and your land will be married. ⁵ As a young man marries a maiden, so will your sons marry you; as a bridegroom rejoices over his bride, so will your God rejoice over you. ⁶ I have posted watchmen on your walls, O Jerusalem; they will never be silent day or night. You who call on the LORD, give yourselves no rest, ⁷ and give him no rest till he establishes Jerusalem and makes her the praise of the earth. ⁸ The LORD has sworn by his right hand and by his mighty arm: "Never again will I give your grain as food for your enemies, and never again will foreigners drink the new wine for which you have toiled; ⁹ but those who harvest it will eat it and praise the LORD, and those who gather the grapes will drink it in the courts of my sanctuary." ¹⁰ Pass through, pass through the gates! Prepare the way for the people. Build up, build up the highway! Remove the stones. Raise a banner for the nations. ¹¹ The LORD has made proclamation to the ends of the earth: "Say to the Daughter of Zion, 'See, your Savior comes! See, his reward is with him, and his recompense accompanies him.'" ¹² They will be called the Holy People, the Redeemed of the LORD; and you will be called Sought After, the City No Longer Deserted.

(NIV)

© Belonging to Him Ministries 2009. All rights reserved.

Sitting in Isaiah

Chapter Nine　　　　　　　　　　　　　　　　　　　　　　　　　　　**Lesson One**

Read Isaiah 62. **Key Verses Isaiah 62:2-4a** "The nations will see your righteousness, and all kings your glory; you will be called by a new name that the mouth of the LORD will bestow. You will be a crown of splendor in the LORD's hand, a royal diadem in the hand of your God. No longer will they call you Deserted, or name your land Desolate." **Review** this week's key verses and write them on an index card to carry with you to review throughout the day and week.

Have you ever watched someone get a "make-over"? There was a television show that my employer was represented on and so I was required to watch *What Not To Wear*. It was horrifying to watch as so called "friends" would nominate their friend (who they believed to be in need of an updated look and wardrobe) to come on the show and basically be completely humiliated by the cast. Not only do they open up the poor soul's closet to the entire world to see, but they make fun and comedy over their wardrobe pieces. The contestants have to participate in modeling their old clothing articles that are soon to be rejected and cast off to the garbage. Some contestants were obviously wounded as some of their favorite pieces were being thrown away.

Some of us feel like our everyday life is the show *What Not to Wear*, except we aren't necessarily being rejected for our outward image as much as we are continually rejected and degraded for who we are on the inside. We primarily do this to ourselves, and occasionally we allow others to join the show. Often we actually take comfort and pleasure in self-rejection, degrading and debasing ourselves, even though we may not always be conscious of what we are doing. We often expect to be rejected, so we self-sabotage to induce and control rejection. Many find rejection more comfortable than acceptance because self-acceptance is alien to the soul.

Do you struggle with degrading thoughts and self-rejection? Do you expect rejection and sometimes sabotage situations to control rejection? At times are you more comfortable with rejection than acceptance?

Sitting in Isaiah

Having a poor self-image (the mental picture of yourself that you carry around) and being confused about who you are is a common struggle that if left unresolved will bring desolation and ruination to our soul. For decades our society has emphasized the importance of having a healthy self-image. Psychologists help people develop a new mental picture of themselves to carry around inside, but they have only begun to do something that God has been working on since the fall of Adam and Eve.

This week we are going to learn *What Not to Wear*, but it will have nothing to do with our outward appearance and earthly rags and everything to do with our inward self, our soul. Through Isaiah 62 we will discover God's "Soul Make-over", our new identity. Dear Beloved, this work will likely take you out of your comfort zone and the success you achieve will correlate directly to your cooperation and participation. I ask you to trust me as we journey together to unearth a new you, a new image and a new identity.

Take a fresh look at Isaiah 62. As you read ask yourself "what truths from Isaiah 62 especially minister to my sense of who I am? Write out several "I am" statements about yourself from Isaiah 62 in the space below. Example: "I am righteous like the dawn" (verse 1).

Optional reading assignment for today: Isaiah Chapter 53.

© Belonging to Him Ministries 2009. All rights reserved.

Sitting in Isaiah

Chapter Nine   **Lesson Two**

Read Isaiah 62 out loud. **Review** this week's key verses Isaiah 62:2-4a. Read today's focus verses Isaiah 62:1-5 and take note of everything God did to give Israel a new identity. Notice the new names God gave Israel: Hephzibah (khef-tsee'baw) means my delight is in her and Beulah (byu-law) means to marry or be married.

"God puts such great emphasis on our self-concept because we act like the person we see ourselves to be. A small self-image sets boundaries on what we can accomplish. A negative self-image predisposes us to failure and unhappiness. An inflated self-image makes us our own worst enemy in relating to other people. A changed self-image—one that is transformed by God—can alter our personality and behavior in delightful ways" (Myers, *Christ Life*, pp. 6-7).

We nurture and develop a poor self-image over time because most of us base our worth on the wrong things.
- Satan's lies

- our own past experiences

- our feelings (instead of on the solid, glorious, scriptural facts of who God is, what He has accomplished and who we are in Him

- people's reactions to us and comments made that are formational in helping to solidify our own negative or positive mental picture of our self. (Myers, *Christ Life*, p. 11)

On which one of these lies do you tend to base your self-image? Reflect on how you have done this in the past. Give an example below.

© Belonging to Him Ministries 2009. All rights reserved.

Sitting in Isaiah

Part of our faulty self-image is that we base our self worth on the world's value system rather than God's. By basing our self worth on our **appearance, performance or status** we are buying into Satan's lies and basing who we are on how we rate in each one of these areas. By doing this we are chasing a moving target because standards of excellence and achievement are always moving and changing. If we base our worth on appearance it's a losing battle because our appearance changes as we age.

Many seek to gain support for their self-image through performing. Performance brings attention and perhaps even encouragement to continue basing worth in that performance because a need for affirmation and attention is being met when you perform.

The value of status in our society is over the top. The Hollywood mentality of worshiping those who are powerful because they are wealthy, beautiful (sometimes though not always) and famous has caused extensive damage to our self-worth. Many prioritize status over everything. For some, it's the status symbols that give value to life such as the cars, houses, clothing, accessories, vacations, social contacts, education and even children.

In what ways have you based your self image on your appearance, performance or status (Myers, *Christ Life*, p. 61)?

Sitting in Isaiah

We can't build a positive self-image just through *the power of positive thinking* alone, because there is no lasting power in only thinking positive thoughts for the sake of positive thinking. But when we combine who God says He is in His Word with who He says we are in His Word, we then have a powerful life changing image transforming thought that is based on a sure foundation of truth. By focusing on who we are according to God, we can begin to reform our image and create new mental pictures of who we truly are. By understanding God's view of us we build a stable new identity of emotional security.

Spend time in quiet reflection asking God to reveal to you your negative self-image. As images come to mind, confess them as sin and ask Him to replace them with powerful life-changing, image-transforming thoughts.

Write these new positive truth thoughts about yourself in the space below and then record your holy conversation. If this area of negative self-image is a struggle for you, consider writing some of the truths about yourself on index cards to carry with you and review throughout the day. End your time in praise and thanksgiving to redirect your thoughts and refocus your emotions. Be encouraged, Beloved. Isaiah 62 is proof that God specializes in rebuilding ruined lives.

Optional reading assignment for today: Isaiah Chapter 54.

Sitting in Isaiah

Chapter Nine   **Lesson Three**

Read all of Isaiah 62 in your favorite translation and **review** this week's key verse Isaiah 62:2-4a by writing it from memory. Read today's focus verses 1-5 & 12 and substitute your name in the passage so that everything God did for Zion, or Jerusalem He has also done for you (Because He has!). What truth has God demonstrated for you from Isaiah 62 that you are most thankful for today and why?

Chapter 62 opens up with a great promise from our Father God as He promises to continue to keep speaking and working until His plans and purposes for you are accomplished. He never gives up, no matter what. He never gives up on you, your life, on your loved ones or your enemies. His specialty is rebuilding broken ruined lives.

Throughout Isaiah God works to transform Israel's self image so that she would begin to act like who she was created to be. The same is true for us, God wants us to be who we are created to be and behave in a "manner worthy of the Lord, pleasing Him in all respects, bearing fruit in every good work and increasing in the knowledge of God; (Colossians 1:10, THE MESSAGE). You are God's daughter and if you aren't behaving that way, it's probably because you don't really believe you are who He says you are. Selected verses from Isaiah 62 from *The Message* are written below. Read them and see how precious you are to God.

> *"You are a stunning crown in the palm of God's hand like a jeweled gold cup held high in the hand of your God. You are so bright people won't be able to help but notice and they will need shades to look at you! He is so proud of you. No more will anyone call you Rejected, and your country will no more be called Ruined. Your new name is His Delight and Married because from now on you are a place of new beginnings, a place*

Sitting in Isaiah

ideal for wedding celebrations. Just like a young man marries his virgin bride, so your builder (God) marries you, and as a bridegroom is happy in his bride, so your God is happy with you" (adapted from the THE MESSAGE).

One way to create new powerful life-changing, image-transforming thoughts is to personalize the following verses by inserting your name. Rewrite them in a personal prayer to God asking Him to make every one of them true for you so that you will experience them in your heart.

I Samuel 2:8 says "He raises the poor from the dust and lifts the needy from the ash heap; he seats them with princes and has them inherit a throne of honor."

Ephesians 4:4 says "Long before he laid down earth's foundations, he had (me) in mind, had settled on (me) as the focus of his love, to be made whole and holy by his love. Long, long ago he decided to adopt (me) into his family through Jesus Christ. (What pleasure he took in planning this!) He wanted (me) to enter into the celebration of his lavish gift-giving by the hand of his beloved Son" (THE MESSAGE).

Sitting in Isaiah

Romans 8:35-39 says "Do you think anyone is going to be able to drive a wedge between (you) and Christ's love for (you)? There is no way! Not trouble, not hard times, not hatred, not hunger, not homelessness, not bullying threats, not backstabbing, not even the worst sins listed in Scripture…none of this fazes (me) because Jesus loves (me) …absolutely nothing can get between (me) and God's love because of the way that Jesus (my) Master has embraced (me)" (THE MESSAGE).

Optional reading assignment for today: Isaiah Chapter 56.

© Belonging to Him Ministries 2009. All rights reserved.

Sitting in Isaiah

Chapter Nine   **Lesson Four**

Read all of Isaiah 62 from your favorite translation. **Review** this week's key verse Isaiah 62:2-4a by saying it out loud from memory. Review today's focus verses, Isaiah 62:6-9.

My father was a pastor and also worked as a local fireman. Both vocations save people from burning to death. One saves souls from the Lake of Fire and the other saves people from burning buildings.

As a fireman's daughter I had the privilege of access to the firehouse. Going with my Dad to the firehouse was one of the most exciting things for me because as my Daddy's daughter I was treated like royalty. At the firehouse I felt special. I was allowed to go into the house and see and touch anything I wanted to. I could climb on the trucks and ride up front on the hook and ladder trucks in parades. I was special and privileged because of who my Daddy was.

This is true for us if we belong to God. We have access to Him because of Jesus. But many of us don't enjoy the benefits of belonging to Him. Instead we live like Cinderella with a Cinderella mentality. We work hard for God and just like Cinderella we bear most of the responsibility, but don't enjoy any of the reward or access of being His. Many of us live like a gardener who works hard to keep the grounds beautiful and well manicured but are never invited inside the house. The gardener sees in the windows of the house of the life within. He watches the Father enjoying life in the house with his family, but the gardener isn't allowed inside because he isn't part of the family. We aren't to be living as a Cinderella or a gardener. We are a daughter and we have access to our Father and His house because we belong to Him. To belong means to be accepted, be in the right place and be a part of something. We can fit in with God and know that we are in the right place, the place of belonging and have full access to Him.

Do you relate to the analogy of having a Cinderella or gardener mentality? If so, record how you see this played out in your life?

Access means to have the means to enter or approach, the right to experience or make use of something and have contact. *"Through him (Christ) we both (Christ and us)…have equal access to the Father."* (Ephesians 2:18, THE MESSAGE) We live in God's presence every moment of everyday because of Jesus. *"We throw open our doors to God and discover at the same moment that he has already thrown open his door to us." We find ourselves standing*

© Belonging to Him Ministries 2009. All rights reserved.

Sitting in Isaiah

where we always hoped we might stand—out in the wide open spaces of God's grace and glory." (Romans 5:2, *THE MESSAGE*)   Access means privilege. *"So let's walk right up to him and get what he is so ready to give. Take the mercy and accept the help."* (Hebrews 4:16, *THE MESSAGE*)

We were made to belong, so if we feel that we don't fit in or belong we will find something to belong to, even if it is entirely the wrong thing!

What kinds of things do you try to fit in to or belong to in order to meet this need?

Often we have feelings that aren't true because our thoughts aren't true. Sometimes we feel like we don't fit in or aren't accepted because we are looking for acceptance from the wrong things. If we rely on worldly values to give us a sense of belonging we will always feel insecure. The only way we can find security and a sense of belonging is to access our Heavenly Father and spend time getting connected to Him.

Reflect on these truths, ask God to reveal truth about your inner self to you through the Spirit and confess what you discover to be true about yourself. Write a prayer asking God to heal your negative self-image and begin to create new positive images to post in your inner photo album.

Optional reading assignment for today: Isaiah Chapter 58.

© Belonging to Him Ministries 2009. All rights reserved.

Sitting in Isaiah

Chapter Nine   **Lesson Five**

Read Isaiah 62 out loud. **Review** this week's key verse from memory, Isaiah 62:2-4a. Read today's focus verses 6-7 and notice the use of the word *establish*. Establish means to start or set up something that is intended to continue or be permanent. What truth from Isaiah 62 do you want God to establish in you and make permanent?

The good news in Isaiah 62 is that God isn't looking for perfectly polished people to join his family. God's great love and desire is to rebuild broken people who are willing to surrender everything to Him, even and *especially* the broken pieces of their lives.

Many of us fear we may never experience what it is like to know that we belong to God because we are so badly depleted, drought-stricken and desolate. Our lives look like a multi-car pile up on the freeway of life. We want to be established in God and experience a permanent sense of belonging, but we can't get past our own past. We feel like we just aren't good enough and we've grown accustomed to feeling like an alien and an outsider. Many feel alone at church more then anywhere else because they are ashamed and embarrassed by their issues.

In 2 Corinthians 12:9-10 we see that God wants to set us free, and to not be ashamed of our issues because He allowed our weaknesses so that He could manifest His strength in us. The word weakness from 2 Corinthians 12:9-10 means any limitation that you inherited or have no power to change, like a disease, chronic illness, emotional trauma, abuse, learning disability, your station in your life or family position. None of us were given the choice of what family to be born into (though Lord knows some of us wish we had been!). God placed us in our families as part of His bigger plan for our life, not by accident, but with purpose.

What difficulties have you struggled with that you had no control over that have had a lasting negative impact upon you? If you aren't sure, ask God to show you and record your thoughts below. As you move on from this reflection question you may discover other areas where you feel weak or exposed. Come back to write them down to refer to later.

© Belonging to Him Ministries 2009. All rights reserved.

Sitting in Isaiah

As we come to terms with our weaknesses and vulnerabilities it's important for us to know the following truths:

- God is never limited by our weaknesses.

- Knowing our weaknesses gives opportunity to better depend upon God.

- Being aware of our vulnerabilities helps us resist the attacks of the enemy.

- Knowing our weaknesses and limitations increases our capacity to show mercy for others who struggle as we have and thereby give opportunity for ministry.

- Our most effective ministry develops out of our greatest difficulties and deepest hurts.

- Being real about our issues helps protect us from becoming prideful.

- Being real with God and others removes the barriers to fellowship and genuine connection.

What truth from the list above do you struggle to believe, experience or live out in your life? Write a prayer asking God to permanently establish these truths in you along with a sense of belongingness that is based on the sure foundation of truth. Thank Him in advance for He always answers prayers that draw us closer to Him.

"I quit focusing on the handicap and began appreciating the gift. It was a case of Christ's strength moving in on my weakness. Now I take limitations in stride, and with good cheer, these limitations that cut me down to size—abuse, accidents, opposition, bad breaks. I just let Christ take over! And so the weaker I get, the stronger I become" (2 Corinthians 12:10, THE MESSAGE).

Optional reading assignment for today: Isaiah Chapter 59.

© Belonging to Him Ministries 2009. All rights reserved.

Chapter Ten

Isaiah 35

Sitting in Isaiah

Isaiah 35

Joy of the Redeemed

The desert and the parched land will be glad; the wilderness will rejoice and blossom. Like the crocus, [2] it will burst into bloom; it will rejoice greatly and shout for joy. The glory of Lebanon will be given to it, the splendor of Carmel and Sharon; they will see the glory of the LORD, the splendor of our God. [3] Strengthen the feeble hands, steady the knees that give way; [4] say to those with fearful hearts, "Be strong, do not fear; your God will come, he will come with vengeance; with divine retribution he will come to save you. [5] Then will the eyes of the blind be opened and the ears of the deaf unstopped. [6] Then will the lame leap like a deer, and the mute tongue shout for joy. Water will gush forth in the wilderness and streams in the desert. [7] The burning sand will become a pool, the thirsty ground bubbling springs. In the haunts where jackals once lay, grass and reeds and papyrus will grow. [8] And a highway will be there; it will be called the Way of Holiness. The unclean will not journey on it; it will be for those who walk in that Way; wicked fools will not go about on it. [9] No lion will be there, nor will any ferocious beast get up on it; they will not be found there. But only the redeemed will walk there [10] and the ransomed of the LORD will return. They will enter Zion with singing; everlasting joy will crown their heads. Gladness and joy will overtake them, and sorrow and sighing will flee away.

(NIV)

Sitting in Isaiah

Chapter Ten   **Lesson One**

Read Isaiah 35. **Key Verses Isaiah 35:3-4** "Strengthen the feeble hands, steady the knees that give way; say to those with fearful hearts, "Be strong, do not fear; your God will come, he will come with vengeance; with divine retribution he will come to save you". **Review** this week's key verses and write them on an index card to carry with you to review throughout the week. Our key verses for this week are so encouraging. Think of being strengthened and steadied as we wait on God. What are you waiting on God to do in your life? What is weighing you down and threatening to rob you of your joy and peace? Explain below. Write a prayer asking God to strengthen and steady you through your time in Isaiah 35 as you wait for Him to show Himself to you in your situation.

Isaiah 35 is known as the Song of the Redeemed and fits so well as our last chapter to study in Sitting in Isaiah. It is the promise of a bright future, even though our present may not look so promising. In verse one the blossoming desert vegetation is a symbol of the inward change that happens in the redeemed soul. The good news we have experienced throughout Isaiah is that "God starts His renewing work of grace in the desert of our real lives". (Ortlund, p. 201)

Are you experiencing new life in your desert as Isaiah discusses in verses 1-2? What kind of new growth do you see happening in you?

© Belonging to Him Ministries 2009. All rights reserved.

Sitting in Isaiah

To remain refreshed, renewed and restored we must protect our souls from the harsh elements of the world. One of God's primary defenses for our protection is encouragement. To encourage means to assist with something or to give support that inspires *courage, confidence and hope* in someone or something. "Encouragement is one of the most important ways God spreads His goodness in our direction (2 Corinthians 1:3-7). He wants us to encourage one another to look for new blessings from Him." (Ortlund, p. 201) Encouragement is two-way; we need to be encouraged and we need to encourage others, not just because it's a nice thing to do, but because God commands it.

When we receive Christ as our Savior the Holy Spirit imparts to us spiritual gifts for the purpose of serving the body of Christ and evangelizing the world (Romans 12). There is an individual spiritual gift of encouragement that is given by the Holy Spirit (Romans 12:8). We don't all have the spiritual gift of encouragement, but every believer is commanded to encourage others. God's Word is clear that we are to encourage and build each other up especially the weak and timid (1 Thessalonians 5:1, 14). We are to do this for each other daily, as long as we still have today (Hebrews 3:13)!

When you are discouraged and in need of encouragement, what helps to lift you up, refocus your attention on God and choose joy?

Who have you recently encouraged to remain faithful while they wait on God to move in their difficulties and answer their prayers? Write a prayer for them below and keep up the good work of strengthening and steadying them! (Hebrews 10:2-25, THE MESSAGE)

Optional reading assignment for today: Isaiah Chapter 60.

© Belonging to Him Ministries 2009. All rights reserved.

Sitting in Isaiah

Chapter Ten   **Lesson Two**

Read Isaiah 35 out loud. **Review** this week's key verses Isaiah 35:3-4. Read today's focus verses Isaiah 35:1-7.

Isaiah 35 is an exciting passage revealing God's plan for spiritual wellness and healthy souls. Part of His plan revealed in Isaiah 35 is not only for encouragement as we discussed yesterday but for literal physical help. Everyone needs a hand now and then, even leaders. Leaders are servers, so if you are serving in some capacity (home, church, school, work, community or nationally) then you are a leader.

In Isaiah 35:4 the open hand is the same phrase open hand used in Exodus 17:11. Moses was leading the Israelites with the help of Joshua and Aaron. In Exodus 17:8-15 the Israelites were battling against the Amalekites under Joshua's leadership. Moses stood upon a hill watching the battle below. As he kept his hands raised toward heaven the Israelites were winning, but when he would succumb to the fatigue and drop his hands they would begin to loose the battle. Aaron and Hur gave him a stone to sit on so he could rest his legs and proceeded to hold his arms up for him through the remainder of the battle. *"One on one side and one on the other –so that his (Moses') hands remained steady (all day) till sunset"!* Israel won the battle that day.

Every one needs support and encouragement to complete the call God has placed upon us. While it is true that at times we are called to solitude for the purpose of prayer and meditation we are also called to have support, connection and relationships. No one is called to walk alone. Who walks beside you Dear One? Think about those who have helped to strengthen, steady and encourage you in your walk with Christ. Make a list below and thank God for each of them. If you are in need of someone to walk with you, ask God to provide that person for you.

Read on in Exodus 18 and see that not only did Moses surround himself with the support and accountability of godly companions, but he also had a spiritual mentor named Jethro who was a priest from Midian and also his father-in-law. In Exodus 18:17 Jethro pays Moses a visit and offers him some sound advice after observing that Moses had taken on too much by himself and was wearing himself out. Moses not only listens to Jethro taking his words to heart but also follows his advice. Moses responds to the advice of his mentor and makes a leadership course

Sitting in Isaiah

correction by delegating some of his responsibilities. He enlists the help of other leaders to share in the responsibility of leading the people and to use their gifting. This strengthened the community as more people had a sense of belonging and ownership.

No matter how old we are or how long we have known Christ we never out grow our need to have or be a mentor. A mentor is an experienced adviser, supporter or trainer who gives guidance and advice to a younger, less experienced person.

Everyone has had or is a mentor in one way or the other. By the time the average person reaches the age of 40 they will have had at least 40 mentors. Our first mentors are our parents, grandparents, aunts and uncles, care-givers and siblings. Our spouses, teachers, scout leaders, Sunday school teachers, pastors, coaches, trainers, team captains, youth leaders, Bible study leaders, employers, co-workers, doctors, lawyers, friends and neighbors all have been mentors to us at one time or another. Some mentors come into our life for only a brief time to serve a specific purpose and then we grow apart again. Some mentors are connected to us for most of our lives.

Make a list of those individuals who have mentored you, even when you weren't aware that you were being taught or helped. Reflect on those who had the most influence on you and why. What did they do differently that helped make a difference for you?

Consider writing a note of thanks to those special mentors who helped shape you into the person you are today.

Optional reading assignment for today: Isaiah Chapter 63.

© Belonging to Him Ministries 2009. All rights reserved.

Sitting in Isaiah

Chapter Ten   **Lesson Three**

Read all of Isaiah 35 in your favorite translation and **review** this week's key verse Isaiah 35:3-4 by writing it from memory. Read today's focus verses 1-7 and take note of the emotional words, like joy, glad, etc. Make a list of all the positive emotional words from verse 1-7 and circle the word "will" every time it appears.

One of the foundational elements in God's health and wellness plan for our soul is praise. Praise is the doorway of joy for our souls. When we open the door of our souls to praise we enter into God's presence immediately for God inhabits the praises of his people (Psalm 22:3). When we praise we are tuning into God, like a radio station we listen to. We praise God by our worship and thanksgiving, recalling His character, remembering what He has done, reminding ourselves of His promises and by believing Him and His Word.

Take a few moments to praise God using the methods stated above. Write a prayer of praise below.

Praise is the key to living a life of steady faith. It is the foundation for which we live refreshed, renewed and fully restored lives. In *Treasury of Praise*, Ruth Myers writes, "It's not that praise is sort of this magical incantation that makes us strong in faith and maneuvers God into doing what we want. Rather, through praise we focus on God. It is a ramp onto the highway of faith and holiness." When we are experiencing difficulties and our faith is being tested, praise

Sitting in Isaiah

changes our soul's climate and atmosphere. In the midst of a struggle, if we can muster up strength to praise God, then even when our circumstances don't change our attitude does, because we begin to see our life through a new pair of lenses. Our change in attitude also influences people around us by bringing peace and hope to others too. When we praise God in the midst of what may feel like defeat we experience real transforming victory because "true praise is unconditional, it helps us accept our situation as it is" (p. 220).

In the past how has praising God helped you see your situation with new lenses? If so, explain below. If not, what are the attitudes that prevented you from practicing praise?

Through praise we activate God's power in our lives. Often God doesn't begin to move in our circumstances until He is finished moving in our heart. When we look up and praise Him, the doorway of our soul is open to Him and His transforming power to do the work necessary for healing. We can experience growth and even profit from our trials through the avenue of praise. "Our praise and thanksgiving can help form a highway—a smooth level road—on which the Lord can ride forth unhindered to deliver and bless. We see this in Psalm 68:4: 'Sing to God, sing praises to His name; lift up a song for Him who rides through the deserts, whose name is the Lord, and exult before Him" (Myers, p. 221). When we praise God despite our difficulties we open our hearts to true humility and a highway to holiness, just as Isaiah 35:8 says, "a highway will be there (in the desert) and it will be called the Way of Holiness."

When we open the door of our souls with praise it's like a stream of water gushing forth in the desert of our lives. Through praise we are refreshed, renewed, restored as God's Spirit pours himself out on us and our desert begins to break forth into new life. Isaiah 35:6 promises that *water will gush forth in the wilderness.* Praise is God's protection from drought and sure destruction and is a sure-fire way to keep us on the highway of holiness.

© Belonging to Him Ministries 2009. All rights reserved.

Sitting in Isaiah

Write a prayer below asking God to create in you a grateful heart that is steady and sure in praising Him everyday for everything, both the good and the bad. Include the good and the bad in your praise prayer below.

Optional reading assignment for today: Isaiah Chapter 64.

Sitting in Isaiah

Chapter Ten   **Lesson Four**

Read all of Isaiah 35 from your favorite translation, asking God to help you to read it with fresh eyes and new insight. **Review** this week's key verse Isaiah 35:3-4 by saying it out loud from memory.

As we conclude our time in the spiritual spa of Isaiah it is important for us to be prepared to live spiritually healthy. If you were preparing to leave an actual physical spa your caretaker would likely be loading you up with all kinds of paperwork and pamphlets with written directions to reinforce all you learned while "spa-ing". Typically a spa would offer you a tailor-made wellness plan, one that took into account not only who you are but a plan that addressed whatever issues you face in your life as well. Hopefully that is what you have gained in your time in this study, and the pages in this book are God's wellness plan for health and vitality of your soul.

- Put on Christ and make him your life (Colossians 3:4). Think of what it means to have Christ as your indwelling life, that God has infused you with the person and life of His son—that something tremendous has taken place deep inside of you! (Myers, *Treasury of Praise*, p.224) Taking in the reality that Christ is your life will help you to live a life of humility and repentance before Jesus everyday. He will begin to transform your character to be like His as you develop more and more spiritual fruit.

- Tap into the power of God's Word by reading it daily. God's word must be the foundation of your wellness. Everything you think, do, say and believe should line up with truth of God's Word. Memorize and meditate on key verses so that God's Word permeates into the depths of your soul. Knowing the Word helps to protect you from toxins polluting your soul and from gaining a stronghold in your life.

- Don't leave room or make provision for the flesh (Romans 13:14). Always put the Spirit of God first and leave your flesh behind. Seek satisfaction in the Spirit and not in the flesh or the things in this world. Develop the discipline of regular prayer and fasting to aid in strengthening your spiritual disciplines.

- Practice the presence of God through the habit of praise. Praise God in everything, choosing joy over despair and hopelessness. Remember that it is a sin to not choose joy even in the midst of pain and trials and allow yourself to sink into despair.

- Be responsible for yourself. Intentionally seek to be filled with the Holy Spirit, remembering that because you are an empty vessel you will naturally get filled up with something, maybe the wrong thing. Love God, others and yourself enough to take care of you. Seek to be filled spiritually, emotionally and physically and ask Him for what you need.

© Belonging to Him Ministries 2009. All rights reserved.

Sitting in Isaiah

- Continue to foster your sense of belonging, identity and self-worth in God, His Word and His love for you. Take great care to not get caught up in seeking self-worth from the world.

- Seek accountability, mentoring, support, prayer and encouragement. If you aren't part of a small group where you receive such support, then find or create one with God's help.

- Serve God and others even during difficult times. When you feel barren consider how you might serve others even if it is serving "light" with ushering, setup/cleanup or helping with coffee service. Encourage others, pray for others and build up others especially when you are down, remembering that when you are serving others you are serving the Lord.

Beloved One, if you are struggling to carry through with the disciplines listed, begin by asking God for the strength to build godly disciplines into your life. Ask in faith and believe that God will answer you. Reflect on how you would start implementing a plan to follow through with these disciplines. Write a prayer of commitment below and ask God to bless your plans.

Optional reading assignment for today: Isaiah Chapter 65.

© Belonging to Him Ministries 2009. All rights reserved.

Sitting in Isaiah

Chapter Ten   **Lesson Five**

Read Isaiah out loud. **Review** this week's key verse from memory, Isaiah 35:3-4. Review today's focus verses, Isaiah 35:8-10 and take note of the description of the highway of holiness. A highway is a raised level mound or way, a main road, a direct route, thoroughfare or freeway that connects a place to a place. Write a description of the highway from today's focus verses. Include in your description the name of the highway, who will and won't be on it, and what life on the highway will be like for those who walk it. Where does the highway lead?

The highway of holiness represents God's pathway to spiritual health. According to Isaiah 40:3, 35:8 and 62:10, a highway will appear in the wilderness for God's people. It is His way to ensure that we live refreshed, renewed and restored as we walk our spiritual journey. It is a roadway through the desert times of our lives so that we can find our way to Him even when we are parched, thirsty and barren. The pathway in our wilderness is an elevated, level, straight roadway that ultimately leads us home to God. On His highway we find a sense of belongingness where we can feel connected in our journey.

On God's roadway we enjoy the fellowship and support of other believers and experience God's protection. We are set apart on the Highway of Holiness as it is reserved and preserved for us, offering us easy and uninterrupted access to God.

We discover God's highway by believing Him and putting our faith and trust in Him alone. Finding the pathway can be easier than staying on the Way. To continue on the road in the wilderness and lush gardens on your spiritual walk means practicing His wellness plan detailed in yesterday's lesson.

Have you found His Highway of Holiness? If so, reflect on what the journey along the Way has been like for you. If not, what do you think is keeping you from discovering His roadway in the desert?

© Belonging to Him Ministries 2009. All rights reserved.

Sitting in Isaiah

Spend some time in quiet reflection and listening prayer before writing out your wellness plan with the help of the Holy Spirit. Use the guidelines offered in yesterday's lesson to help you. End your prayer time today in praise to God for preparing a way for you!

Optional reading assignment for today: Isaiah Chapter 66.

Sitting in Isaiah

Additional Notes

Sitting in Isaiah

Bibliography

Alsdorf, Debbie. *A Different Kind of Wild*,

Bright, Bill. *Your Personal Guide to Fasting and Prayer*, www.ccci.org

Lockyer, Herbert, Sr., gen. ed. *Nelson's Illustrated Bible Dictionary*. Nashville: Thomas Nelson Publishers, 1986.

Lucado, Max. *It's Not About Me*. Nashville: Integrity Publishers, 2004.

Minter, Kelly. *No Other Gods*. Colorado Springs: David C Cook, 2008.

Moore, Beth. *Get Out of that Pit: Straight Talk about God's Deliverance*. Nashville: Integrity Publishers, 2007.

Moore, Beth. *Praying God's Word: Breaking Free from Spiritual Strongholds*. Nashville: Broadman and Holman Publishers, 2000.

Meyer, Joyce. *Battlefield of the Mind: Winning the Battle in Your Mind*. Tulsa, Harrison House, 1995.

Myers, Ruth. *Christ/Life*. Sisters, Oregon: Multnomah Publishers, 2005.

Myers, Ruth and Warren. *A Treasury of Praise: Enjoying God Anew*. Colorado Springs: Multnomah Books, 2007.

Myers, Ruth and Warren. *31 Days of Praise: Enjoying God Anew*. Sisters, Oregon: Multnomah Publishers, 1994.

Myers, Ruth and Warren. *31 Days of Prayer: Moving God's Mighty Hand*. Sisters, Oregon: Multnomah Publishers, 1997.

Myers, Ruth and Warren. *31 Days of Power: Learning to live in Spiritual Victory*. Sisters, Oregon: Multnomah Publishers, 2003.

Ortlund, Raymond C., Jr. *Isaiah: God Saves Sinners*. Wheaton: Crossway Books, 2005.

Ryrie, Charles C. *The Ryrie Study Bible*. Chicago, Illinois: Moody Press, 1976.

Sailhamer, John H. *The Pentateuch as Narrative*. Grand Rapids, Michigan: Zondervan, 1992.

Vigliano, Joe. *A Prayer for Spiritual Warfare*. http://www.focus-on-prayer.com/Spiritual-Warfare-Prayer.html

Wiersbe, Warren W. *The Bible Exposition Commentary: Prophets*. Colorado Springs: Victor, 2002.

© Belonging to Him Ministries 2009. All rights reserved.

www.ingramcontent.com/pod-product-compliance
Lightning Source LLC
Chambersburg PA
CBHW080508110426
42742CB00017B/3043